Advancing Maths for AQA
STATISTICS 7

Roger Williamson and John White

Series editors
Roger Williamson   Sam Boardman
Ted Graham   Keith Parramore

1 Linear combinations of independent normal variables   1

2 The exponential distribution   15

3 Estimation   25

4 Hypothesis testing: one-sample tests   35

5 Hypothesis testing: two-sample tests   55

6 Testing for goodness of fit   79

7 Testing the parameter β of the regression equation   103

Exam style practice paper   117

Appendix   121

Answers   133

Index   145

Heinemann Educational Publishers
a division of Heinemann Publishers (Oxford) Ltd,
Halley Court, Jordan Hill, Oxford OX2 8EJ

OXFORD JOHANNESBURG BLANTYRE MELBOURNE
AUCKLAND IBADAN GABORONE PORTSMOUTH NH (USA)
CHICAGO

New material © Roger Williamson and John White
Existing material © CIMT 1994

First published in 2002

06 05 04 03 02
10 9 8 7 6 5 4 3 2 1

ISBN 0 435 51322 2

Cover design by Miller, Craig and Cocking

Typeset and illustrated by Tech-Set Limited, Gateshead, Tyne & Wear

Printed and bound by Scotprint, Haddington, East Lothian

Acknowledgements
The publishers and authors acknowledge the work of the writers David
Burghes and Nigel Price of the *AEB Mathematics for AS and A Level* Series from
which some exercises and examples have been taken.

The publishers' and authors' thanks are due to the AQA for the permission to
reproduce questions from past examination papers.

The answers have been provided by the authors and are not the responsibility
of the examining board.

About this book

This book is one in a series of textbooks designed to provide you with exceptional preparation for AQA's new Advanced GCE Specification B. The series authors are all senior members of the examining team and have prepared the textbooks specifically to support you in studying this course.

Finding your way around

The following are there to help you find your way around when you are studying and revising:

- **edge marks** (shown on the front page) – these help you to get to the right chapter quickly;
- **contents list** – this identifies the individual sections dealing with key syllabus concepts so that you can go straight to the areas that you are looking for;
- **index** – a number in bold type indicates where to find the main entry for that topic.

Key points

Key points are not only summarised at the end of each chapter but are also boxed and highlighted within the text like this:

> A linear combination of independent normal variables will itself be normally distributed.

Exercises and exam questions

Worked examples and carefully graded questions familiarise you with the specification and bring you up to exam standard. Each book contains:

- Worked examples and Worked exam questions to show you how to tackle typical questions; Examiner's tips will also provide guidance;
- Graded exercises, gradually increasing in difficulty up to exam-level questions, which are marked by an [A];
- Test-yourself sections for each chapter so that you can check your understanding of the key aspects of that chapter and identify any sections that you should review;
- Answers to the questions are included at the back of the book.

1 Linear combinations of independent normal variables

Learning objectives	1
1.1 Introduction	1
1.2 Summary of results from S1 and S4	1
1.3 Further results for mean and variance	2
Key point summary	13
Test yourself	13

2 The exponential distribution

Learning objectives	15
2.1 Introduction	15
2.2 The cumulative distribution function	16
2.3 Fitting an exponential distribution	20
Key point summary	23
Test yourself	23

3 Estimation

Learning objectives	25
3.1 Introduction	25
3.2 Confidence intervals for a normal population variance and standard deviation	25
Key point summary	32
Test yourself	32

4 Hypothesis testing: one-sample tests

Learning objectives	34
4.1 Introduction	34
4.2 Normal population variance	36
4.3 Binomial population proportion	38
4.4 Poisson population mean	43
Key point summary	51
Test yourself	52

5 Hypothesis testing: two-sample tests

Learning objectives	55
5.1 Introduction	55
5.2 Two normal population variances	55
5.3 Two normal population means – case 1	59
Independent samples and known population variances – normal test	59

5.4 Two normal population means – case 2   64
     Independent samples and unknown but equal
     population variances – *t*-test   64
     Key point summary   75
     Test yourself   76

6 Testing for goodness of fit
Learning objectives   79
6.1 Introduction   79
6.2 Goodness of fit for discrete distributions   80
6.3 Goodness of fit for continuous distributions   87
     Key point summary   100
     Test yourself   101

7 Testing the parameter β of the regression equation
Learning objectives   103
7.1 Introduction   103
7.2 The simple linear regression model   103
7.3 Testing hypotheses about β   105
     Key point summary   114
     Test yourself   114

Exam style practice paper   117

Appendix
Table 1 Binomial distribution function   121
Table 2 Poisson distribution function   126
Table 3 Normal distribution function   127
**Table 4 Percentage points of the normal
distribution**   128
**Table 5 Percentage points of the student's
t-distribution**   129
Table 6 Percentage points of the χ^2-distribution   130
Table 7 Percentage points of the *F*-distribution   131

Answers   133

Index   145

Linear combinations of independent normal variables

Learning objectives

After studying this chapter you should be able to:

- derive the mean of a linear combination of random variables
- derive the standard deviation (and variance) of a linear combination of independent random variables
- solve problems involving linear combinations of independent, normally distributed, random variables.

1.1 Introduction

You have already met continuous distributions in S1 chapter 7 (the normal distribution) and in S4 chapter 1. The next section summarises some results from these chapters. This chapter then goes on to deal with further results on the mean and variance of random variables. Finally it examines the distribution of a linear combination of independent normal variables.

1.2 Summary of results from S1 and S4

For a continuous distribution, probability is represented by the area under a curve (called the probability density function).

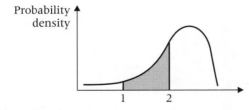

The probability that an observation, selected at random from the distribution, lies between 1 and 2 is represented by the shaded area. Note that the probability that an observation from a continuous distribution is exactly equal to 2 (or any other value) is zero.

There are two conditions for a curve to be used as a probability density function:

- the total area under the curve must be 1,
- the curve must not take negative values, i.e. it must not go below the horizontal axis.

$$E(X) = \int x\,f(x)\,dx$$

where $f(x)$ is the probability density function and the range of integration is the range of values for which $f(x)$ is defined.

> You will not need to use integration in this chapter.

The expectation of $g(X)$, where $g(X)$ is any function of X, is given by

$$E[g(X)] = \int g(x)\,f(x)\,dx.$$

The mean of X is $E(X)$.

The variance of X, $Var(X) = E[\{X - E(X)\}^2] = E(X^2) - [E(X)]^2$.

1.3 Further results for mean and variance

The following results apply to expectations of both discrete and continuous random variables. The proofs, although not difficult, have been omitted. You may be required to use these results but you will not be required to prove them.

Result 1. $E(a + bX) = a + bE(X)$

where a and b are constants and X is a random variable.

> No assumption about the distribution of X is necessary.

For example, the time, in hours, taken by a plumber to deal with a household emergency may be modelled by a random variable, X, with mean 1.7. The plumber's time is charged at £40X plus a callout fee of £48. That is, £$(48 + 40X)$ in total.

The mean charge is

$$E(48 + 40X) = 48 + 40E(X)$$
$$= 48 + 40 \times 1.7 = £116$$

$$E(a + bX) = a + bE(X)$$

Result 2. $E(X + Y) = E(X) + E(Y)$

where X and Y are random variables.

> This applies whether or not X and Y are independent.

For example, the time taken travelling to and from a household emergency by the plumber referred to above can be modelled by a random variable Y with mean 0.9 hours.

The total time spent on the emergency by the plumber is $X + Y$.

The mean of this total time is

$$E(X + Y) = E(X) + E(Y)$$
$$= 1.7 + 0.9 = 2.6 \text{ hours}$$

> *X* is the time for the plumber to deal with the emergency.

$$E(X + Y) = E(X) + E(Y)$$

These two results may be extended to the following more general form.

Result 3. $\mathbf{E(a_0 + a_1 X_1 + a_2 X_2 + \ldots + a_n X_n)}$
$$\mathbf{= a_0 + a_1 E(X_1) + a_2 E(X_2) + \ldots + a_n E(X_n)}$$

where $X_1, X_2, \ldots, X_n$ are random variables and $a_0, a_1, \ldots, a_n$ are constants.

> Again it does not matter whether the random variables are independent or not.

For example, the plumber referred to above also charges the cost of materials used. The cost of materials for each emergency may be modelled by a random variable Z with mean £8. Thus the total charge is $£(48 + 40X + Z)$. The mean total charge is

$$E(48 + 40X + Z) = 48 + 40E(X) + E(Z)$$
$$= 48 + 40 \times 1.7 + 8 = £124$$

$E(a_0 + a_1 X_1 + a_2 X_2 + \ldots + a_n X_n)$
$= a_0 + a_1 E(X_1) + a_2 E(X_2) + \ldots + a_n E(X_n)$

where $X_1, X_2, \ldots, X_n$ are random variables and $a_0, a_1, \ldots, a_n$ are constants.

EXERCISE 1A

1 $E(X) = 6$, $E(Y) = 8$ and $E(Z) = 10$.
Evaluate:
(a) $E(X + Y)$,
(b) $E(X + Y + Z)$,
(c) $E(Z - X)$,
(d) $E(3X)$,
(e) $E(2 - 3X)$,
(f) $E(4Y - 7)$,
(g) $E(7X + 3.5Y - 7 + 4.2Z)$,
(h) $E(0.5X + 1.4Y + 3.2Z)$,
(i) $E(2X - 3Y - 2.5Z + 2)$,
(j) $E(-2 + X - Y + 2Z - 4)$.

Result 4. $\mathbf{Var(a + bX) = b^2\, Var(X)}$

where a and b are constants.

For example, if the time X referred to above had standard deviation 1.9 hours, then the cost, £$(48 + 40X)$ for the plumber's time would have variance

$$40^2 \text{Var}(X) = 40^2 \times 1.9^2 = 5776.$$

The standard deviation of the cost is $\sqrt{5776} = £76$.

> The standard deviation is $40 \times$ (standard deviation of X).

$$\text{Var}(a + bX) = b^2 \text{Var}(X)$$

> The addition of a constant (in this case 48) has no effect on variability.

If X and Y are **independent random** variables

Result 5. $\mathbf{Var(X \pm Y) = Var(X) + Var(Y)}$

Note 1. Unlike the earlier results this only applies if X and Y are independent.

Note 2. At first sight it might seem surprising that $\text{Var}(X - Y)$ is **not** equal to $\text{Var}(X) - \text{Var}(Y)$. However, if this were the case $X - Y$ would have a negative variance if the variance of Y was greater than the variance of X. This is clearly impossible.

Note 3. This result is one of the main reasons why mathematical statisticians are so fond of using variance rather than standard deviation despite standard deviation being a much better measure of variability. The result above does **not** apply to standard deviations.

For example if the time, X, to deal with an emergency had standard deviation 1.9 hours and the travelling time, Y, had standard deviation 0.6 hours the total time spent dealing with the emergency, $X + Y$, would have variance

$$1.9^2 + 0.6^2 = 3.97.$$

The standard deviation $= \sqrt{3.97} = 1.99$ hours.

> This assumes that the time to deal with an emergency is independent of the travelling time.

$$\text{Var}(X \pm Y) = \text{Var}(X) + \text{Var}(Y)$$

where X and Y are independent random variables.

Results 4 and 5 can be combined into the more general form

$$\text{Var}(a_0 + a_1 X_1 + \ldots + a_n X_n) = a_1{}^2 \text{Var}(X_1) + \ldots + a_n{}^2 \text{Var}(X_n)$$

where $X_1, X_2, \ldots, X_n$ are independent random variables and $a_0, a_1, \ldots, a_n$ are constants.

For example, if the cost, Z, of materials had standard deviation £3.50 and was independent of X, the variance of the total cost would be

$$\begin{aligned} \mathrm{Var}(48 + 40X + Z) &= 40^2\,\mathrm{Var}(X) + \mathrm{Var}(Z) \\ &= 40^2 \times 1.9^2 + 3.5^2 \\ &= 5788.25 \end{aligned}$$

The standard deviation = £76.08

> X and Z must be independent for this to be valid.

> $$\mathrm{Var}(a_0 + a_1 X_1 + \ldots + a_n X_n)$$
> $$= a_1{}^2\,\mathrm{Var}(X_1) + \ldots + a_n{}^2\,\mathrm{Var}(X_n)$$
>
> where $X_1, X_2, \ldots, X_n$ are independent random variables and $a_0, a_1, \ldots, a_n$ are constants.

EXERCISE 1B

1 The random variable X has variance 4 and the independent random variable Y has variance 3. Evaluate the variance of:

(a) $X + Y$,

(b) $X - Y$,

(c) $2X$,

(d) $2 + X$,

(e) $Y - X$,

(f) $3X + 4Y$,

(g) $2X - 3Y - 2$.

2 The random variable X has standard deviation 2 and the independent random variable Y has standard deviation 5. Evaluate the standard deviation of:

(a) $X + Y$,

(b) $X - Y$,

(c) $4X$,

(d) $4 + X$,

(e) $Y - X$,

(f) $2X + 5Y$,

(g) $4X - 7Y + 2$.

3 X, Y and Z are independent random variables with means 2, 3 and 4, respectively, and standard deviation 3, 4 and 5, respectively. Evaluate the mean, variance and standard deviation of:

(a) $Y + Z$,

(b) $3Z$,

(c) $2X + 4$,

(d) $X + Y + Z + 1$,

(e) $0.5X - 1.5Y - 2 + 3Z$.

The results above refer to the mean and variance of linear combinations of independent random variables. There is no restriction on the distribution of the random variables. If the variables are all normally distributed then a linear combination of them will also be normally distributed.

> A linear combination of independent normal variables will itself be normally distributed.

Worked example 1.1$

In the mass production of jars of jam the weight of jam put in each jar is a normally distributed random variable, X, with mean 456 g and standard deviation 4 g. The weight of the jar (including the lid) is an independent normally distributed random variable, Y, with mean 35 g and standard deviation 3 g.

(a) Find the distribution of the total weight of a jar of jam.

A child opens a new jar of jam and takes a spoonful out. The weight of jam in the spoon is a normally distributed random variable, Z, with mean 22 g and standard deviation 2 g. Z is independent of X.

(b) Find the distribution of the weight of jam remaining in the jar.

Solution

(a) The total weight of the jam plus the jar is $X + Y$.
The mean of $X + Y$
$= E(X + Y) = E(X) + E(Y) = 456 + 35 = 491$ g.
The variance of $X + Y = \text{Var}(X) + \text{Var}(Y) = 4^2 + 3^2 = 25$.
The standard deviation will be $\sqrt{25} = 5$ g.

> Don't forget to add variances **not** standard deviations.

Since the two variables are **independently normally** distributed the distribution of the total weight will be **normal** with mean 491 g and standard deviation 5 g.

(b) The weight of jam remaining in the jar is $X - Z$.
The mean is $E(X) - E(Z) = 456 - 22 = 434$ g.

The variance of $X - Z$ is $V(X) + V(Z) = 4^2 + 2^2 = 20$.
The standard deviation is $\sqrt{20} = 4.47$ g.

> Always add variances. Never subtract one from another.

Since X and Z are **independently normally** distributed the distribution of $X - Z$ is **normal** with mean 434 g and standard deviation 4.47 g.

Worked example 1.2$

A machine produces rubber balls whose diameters are normally distributed with mean 5.50 cm and standard deviation 0.08 cm. The balls are packed in cylindrical tubes whose internal diameters are normally distributed with mean 5.70 cm and standard deviation 0.12 cm. If a ball, selected at random, is placed in a tube, selected at random, find the probability that the clearance is between 0.05 cm and 0.25 cm. (The clearance is the internal diameter of the tube minus the diameter of the ball.)

Solution

If X is the diameter of the ball and Y is the diameter of the tube the clearance is $Y - X$. This will be normally distributed with mean $= 5.70 - 5.50 = 0.20$, variance $= 0.08^2 + 0.12^2 = 0.0208$, and standard deviation $= 0.1442$.

$$z_1 = (0.05 - 0.20)/0.1442 = -1.040$$
$$z_2 = (0.25 - 0.20)/0.1442 = 0.347$$

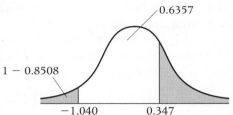

The probability of the clearance between 0.05 cm and 0.25 cm is given by

$$0.6357 - (1 - 0.8508) = 0.4865.$$

Interpolation has been used in reading the normal tables, but the effect on the final answer is small.

> Answers obtained without using interpolation will be accepted in the examination.

Worked example 1.3$

A baker makes digestive biscuits whose weights are normally distributed with mean 24.0 g and standard deviation 1.9 g. The biscuits are packed by hand into packets of 25.

(a) Assuming the biscuits included in each packet are a random sample from the population, what is the distribution of the total weight of biscuits in a packet and what is the probability that it lies between 598 g and 606 g?

(b) Ten packets of biscuits are placed in a box. What is the probability that the total weight of biscuits in the box lies between 6010 g and 6060 g?

(c) A new packer was including 26 biscuits in each packet. What is the probability that a packet selected at random from those containing 25 biscuits would contain a greater weight of biscuit than a packet selected at random from those containing 26 biscuits?

Solution

(a) Since the sample is random the weights of the 25 biscuits included in the packet will be independent of each other. The distribution of the total weight will therefore be normal.

The mean weight of the biscuits in the packet will be
$24 + 24 + \ldots + 24 = 25 \times 24 = 600$ g.

The variance of the total weight will be
$1.9^2 + 1.9^2 + \ldots + 1.9^2 = 25 \times 1.9^2 = 90.25$
giving a standard deviation $= 9.5 \, \text{g}$.

$$z_1 = (598 - 600)/9.5 = -0.211$$
$$z_2 = (606 - 600)/9.5 = 0.632$$

Probability between 598 g and 606 g

$$= 0.7363 - (1 - 0.5836) = 0.320.$$

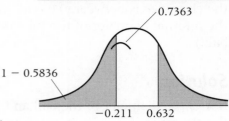

Interpolation has been used in normal tables.

(b) Ten packets of biscuits are placed in a box. Provided their weights are independent the total weight will be normally distributed with mean $10 \times 600 = 6000 \, \text{g}$.
The variance will be $10 \times 90.25 = 902.5$ and the standard deviation $\sqrt{902.5} = 30.04 \, \text{g}$.

$$z_1 = (6010 - 6000)/30.04 = 0.333$$
$$z_2 = (6060 - 6000)/30.04 = 1.997$$

The probability of being between 6010 g and 6060 g

$$= 0.9771 - 0.6304 = 0.347.$$

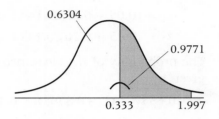

(c) If X is the total weight of biscuits in a packet containing 25 biscuits then we already know that X is N(600, 90.25). If Y is the total weight of biscuits in a packet containing 26 biscuits then Y is normally distributed with mean $26 \times 24 = 624 \, \text{g}$, and variance $26 \times 1.9^2 = 93.86$.
The difference $Y - X$ is normally distributed with

mean $= 624 - 600 = 24 \, \text{g}$,
variance $= 90.25 + 93.86 = 184.11$,
standard deviation $= \sqrt{184.11} = 13.57$.

A packet containing 25 biscuits will weigh more than a packet containing 26 biscuits if $Y - X$ is negative, i.e. $Y - X < 0$,

$$z = (0 - 24)/13.57 = -1.769.$$

The probability of the weight of biscuits in a packet of 25 biscuits exceeding that in a packet of 26 biscuits is $1 - 0.9615 = 0.0385$.

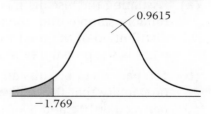

Always add variances.

EXERCISE IC

1 A dispenser discharges an amount of soft drink which is normally distributed with mean 475 ml and standard deviation 20 ml.

(a) State the distribution of the total amount in two independent drinks.

(b) If the capacity of the cups into which the drink is dispensed is normally distributed with mean 500 ml and standard deviation 30 ml, find the distribution of the difference between the capacity of a cup and the amount dispensed.

Assume the capacity of the cup and the amount dispensed are independent.

2 The weights of pieces of home-made fudge are normally distributed with mean 34 g and standard deviation 5 g.

   (a) A bag contains 15 pieces of fudge chosen at random. State the distribution of the total weight of fudge in the bag. Find the probability that the total weight is between 490 g and 540 g.

   (b) Find the probability that the total weight of fudge in a bag containing 15 pieces exceeds that in another bag containing 16 pieces.

3 The weight, X g, of a small bag of crisps is normally distributed with mean 35.5 and variance 0.8. The weight, Y g, of a large bag of crisps is also normally distributed but with mean 152.0 and a variance of 3.2.

   (a) Write down the distribution of $Y - 4X$.

   (b) Hence determine the probability that the weight of a randomly selected large bag of crisps is more than four times the weight of a randomly selected small bag of crisps. [A]

4 Tubes of a particular variety of sweets, when sold individually, have contents whose weights are normally distributed with a mean of 25.8 g and a standard deviation of 1.5 g. Smaller tubes of the same variety of sweets are also sold in multi-packs of five randomly selected tubes. These tubes have contents whose weights are normally distributed with a mean of 20.4 g and a standard deviation of 1.0 g.

   (a) Determine the probability that the weight of the contents of a randomly selected multi-pack exceeds 100 g.

   (b) Determine the probability that the weight of the contents of a randomly selected multi-pack is less than the weight of the contents of four randomly selected tubes which are sold individually.

   (c) Determine the probability that the weight of the contents of a tube, selected at random from a multi-pack, is less than 75 per cent of the weight of the contents of a tube selected at random from those sold individually. [A]

5 Audrey is a regular customer of Toto's taxis. When she rings from home the time, X, a taxi takes to arrive is normally distributed with mean 19 minutes and standard deviation 3 minutes.

(a) (i) Find the probability of her having to wait less than 15 minutes for a taxi.

(ii) What waiting time will be exceeded with probability 0.1?

Audrey decides to try Blue Star taxis. The standard deviation of her waiting time, Y, is 7 minutes and the probability of Y exceeding 8 minutes is 0.977 25.

(b) Find the mean of Y, assuming a normal distribution.

(c) (i) State the distribution of T where $T = X - Y$. (X and Y may be assumed independent.)

(ii) If both firms were rung at the same time, find the probability that Toto would arrive first.

(d) In order to catch a train Audrey needs a taxi within 10 minutes. Which firm would you advise her to ring? Explain your answer. [A]

6 A supermarket stocks two types of bottled water; still and sparkling. During autumn, the daily volume, X l, of still water sold is a normal random variable with mean 86 and standard deviation 15. Independently and during the same period, the daily volume, Y l, of sparkling water sold is also a normal random variable but with mean 72 and standard deviation 10.

(a) State the distribution of $X + Y$, the total amount of bottled water sold during an autumn day.

(b) Hence determine the probability that, during a randomly chosen autumn day, the supermarket sells more than 200 l of bottled water.

(c) Determine the probability that, in total over a five day autumn period, the supermarket sells less than 400 l of still water.

(d) By considering the distribution of $(X - 1.25Y)$, calculate the probability that, on a randomly chosen autumn day, the supermarket sells at least 25 per cent more still water than sparkling water. [A]

7 The thickness of a certain grade of hardboard sheets stocked by a DIY shop is normally distributed with mean 7.3 mm and standard deviation 0.5 mm.

(a) What proportion of sheets will be between 7 mm and 8 mm thick?

(b) Sheets of the same grade bought from a second shop contain 9.0 per cent over 8 mm thick and 2.3 per cent less than 7 mm thick. Assuming that the thickness is normally distributed, find its mean and standard deviation correct to the nearest tenth of a millimetre.

(c) State the distribution of $Y - X$, where X and Y are the thickness of pieces of hardboard selected at random from the first and second shops, respectively. Find the probability that X exceeds Y.

(d) It is possible to buy batches of hardboard from the first shop with any required mean, and with the standard deviation remaining 0.5 mm. What value of the mean should be chosen:
   (i) to minimise the proportion of sheets outside the range 7 mm to 8 mm (no proof required),
   (ii) so that 0.1 per cent of sheets are less than 7 mm thick? [A]

8 A certain brand of beans is sold in tins. The tins are filled and sealed by a machine. The weight of beans in each tin is normally distributed with mean 425 g and standard deviation 25 g, and the weight of the tin is independently normally distributed with mean 90 g and standard deviation 10 g.

(a) Find the probability that the total weight of the sealed tin and its beans:
   (i) exceeds 550 g,
   (ii) lies between 466 g and 575 g.

(b) Calculate an interval within which approximately 90 per cent of the weights of the filled tins will lie.

The tins are packed in boxes of 24. The weight of the box is normally distributed with mean 500 g and standard deviation 30 g.

(c) Find the probability that a full box weighs less than 12.75 kg. [A]

9 Lin Ying belongs to an athletic club. In 800 m races her times are normally distributed with mean 128 s and standard deviation 4 s.

(a) Find the probability of her time in an 800 m race being between 120 and 130 s.

(b) What time will she beat in 70 per cent of her races?

Julie belongs to the same club. In 800 m races 85 per cent of her times are less than 140 s and 70 per cent are less than 135 s. Her times are normally distributed.

(c) Find the mean and standard deviation of Julie's times, each correct to two significant figures.

(d) What is the probability that in an 800 m race Lin Ying will beat Julie?

(e) The club has to choose one of these two athletes to enter a major competition. In order to quality for the final rounds it is necessary to achieve a time of 114 s or less in the heats. Which athlete should be chosen and why? [A]

10 The contents of bags of oats are normally distributed with mean 3.05 kg and standard deviation 0.08 kg.

   (a) Find the proportion of bags which contain less than 3.11 kg.

   (b) Find the proportion of bags which contain between 3.00 and 3.15 kg.

   (c) What weight is exceeded by the contents of 99.9 per cent of the bags?

   (d) If six bags are selected at random, what is the probability that the mean weight of the contents will be between 3.00 and 3.15 kg?

   The weight of the bags when empty is normally distributed with mean 0.12 kg and standard deviation 0.02 kg. Full bags are packed into boxes each of which holds six bags.

   (e) State the distribution of the weight in a box, i.e. six bags together with their contents. Assume that the weight of all bags and contents in a box are independent of each other.

   (f) Within what limits will the weight in a box lie with probability 0.9?   [A]

11 Fertiliser is packed, by a machine, into bags of nominal weight 12 kg. The weight of each bag may be regarded as a normally distributed random variable with mean 12.05 kg and standard deviation 0.20 kg.

   (a) Find the probability that the weight of a bag exceeds 12 kg.

   (b) What weight is exceeded by exactly 95 per cent of the bags?

   A farmer buys 20 bags at a time.

   (c) What is the probability that their mean weight will exceed 12 kg?

   (d) State the distribution of the total weight of the 20 bags and find the probability that it lies between 239.5 kg and 240.5 kg.   [A]

Key point summary

If the letters X and Y are variables and the letters a and b are constants then

1 $E(a + bX) = a + bE(X)$ *p 2*

2 $E(X + Y) = E(X) + E(Y)$ *p 3*

3 $E(a_0 + a_1 X_1 + a_2 X_2 + \ldots + a_n X_n)$ *p 3*
$= a_0 + a_1 E(X_1) + a_2 E(X_2) + \ldots + a_n E(X_n)$

4 $\mathrm{Var}(a + bX) = b^2 \mathrm{Var}(X)$ *p 4*

5 $\mathrm{Var}(X \pm Y) = \mathrm{Var}(X) + \mathrm{Var}(Y)$, if X and Y are   *p 4*
independent.

6 $\mathrm{Var}(a_0 + a_1 X_1 + \ldots + a_n X_n)$ *p 5*
$= a_1^2 \mathrm{Var}(X_1) + \ldots + a_n^2 \mathrm{Var}(X_n)$,
if $X_1, X_2, \ldots, X_n$ are independent.

7 A linear combination of independent normal variables   *p 6*
will itself be normally distributed.

Test yourself	What to review
1 A random variable, X, has mean 4 and variance 25. Evaluate the mean, variance and standard deviation of $2X - 3$.	*Section 1.3*
2 X and Y are independent random variables, each with mean 5 and standard deviation 2. Evaluate the mean and standard deviation of $X - Y$.	*Section 1.3*
3 R is a random variable with mean 4 and variance 9. S is a random variable with mean 5 and variance 16. R and S are not independent. Evaluate, if possible, the mean and standard deviation of: **(a)** $S - R$, **(b)** $4 + S$, **(c)** $5R - 6$.	*Section 1.3*
4 The weights of tins of peas are normally distributed with mean 400 g and standard deviation 12 g. State the distribution of the total weight of a random sample of eight tins.	*Section 1.3*
5 The breaking strains of rope are normally distributed with mean 25 kN and standard deviation 2 kN. During testing a strain is applied. The magnitude of the strain is normally distributed with mean 21 kN and standard deviation 3 kN. Find the probability that in a particular test the strain applied exceeds the breaking strain of a rope. Assume the two are independent.	*Section 1.3*

Test yourself (continued)	**What to review**

6 A machine puts X g of beans in a tin weighing Y g. X and Y are independent random variables with variances 0.16 and 0.09 respectively. The total weight, $Z = X + Y$, is a random variable with variance $0.16 + 0.09 = 0.25$.

Section 1.3

An inspector weighs a large random sample of empty tins and a large random sample of full tins and evaluates the variances of Y and Z. The inspector then argues as follows:

The weight of beans $X = Z - Y$. The variance of the weight of beans is therefore $0.25 + 0.09 = 0.34$.

Explain the fallacy in this argument.

CHAPTER 2

The exponential distribution

Learning objectives

After studying this chapter you should be able to:

■ calculate probabilities from the exponential distribution using the cumulative distribution function

■ use formulae to evaluate the mean and standard deviation (or variance) of an exponential distribution

■ fit an exponential distribution to an observed set of data.

2.1 Introduction

The exponential distribution is a continuous distribution. It is the distribution of the intervals between successive Poisson events. For example, if the number of cars passing a point on a motorway follows a Poisson distribution, the intervals of time between successive cars follow an exponential distribution.

The exponential distribution has probability density function

$$f(x) = \begin{cases} \lambda e^{-\lambda x} & x > 0, \text{ where } \lambda \text{ is a constant} \\ 0 & \text{otherwise} \end{cases}$$

The mean of the exponential distribution is $1/\lambda$.
The standard deviation is also $1/\lambda$.
The variance is $1/\lambda^2$.

These results may be found by integration (see S4 chapter 1). However this module requires polynomial integration only and you will not be asked to derive these results in an examination.

The exponential distribution has probability density function

$$f(x) = \begin{cases} \lambda e^{-\lambda x} & x > 0, \text{ where } \lambda \text{ is a constant} \\ 0 & \text{otherwise} \end{cases}$$

The exponential distribution with parameter λ has mean $1/\lambda$ and standard deviation $1/\lambda$.

2.2 The cumulative distribution function

The probability that an observed value from the exponential distribution is less than x is given by

$$P(X < x) = \int_0^x \lambda e^{-\lambda x}\, dx = [-e^{-\lambda x}]_0^x = 1 - e^{-\lambda x} \qquad x > 0.$$

$P(X < x)$ is known as the cumulative distribution function and is usually denoted $F(x)$.

For the exponential distribution with parameter λ
$F(x) = 1 - e^{-\lambda x} \quad x > 0.$

> You will not be asked to derive this result in an examination.
>
> If $x \leqslant 0$ then $F(x) = 0$. This is of little interest as the exponential distribution cannot take negative values.

The cumulative distribution function may be used as an alternative to integration for evaluating probabilities.

If a and b are two positive constants and a > b, the probability that X takes a value between a and b is

$$P(X < a) - P(X < b) = F(a) - F(b).$$

For example, the interval, X s, between cars passing a point on a motorway follows an exponential distribution with probability density function

$$f(x) = \begin{cases} 2e^{-2x} & x > 0 \\ 0 & \text{otherwise} \end{cases}$$

(Alternatively, this distribution may be described as an exponential distribution with parameter 2.)
The cumulative distribution function is $1 - e^{-2x}$.
The probability that the next interval is between 1 and 2 s is

$$F(2) - F(1) = (1 - e^{-4}) - (1 - e^{-2}) = 0.9817 - 0.8647 = 0.117.$$

> Use your calculator to evaluate e^{-4} and e^{-2}.

The probability that the next interval is longer than 3 s is

$$F(\infty) - F(3) = (1 - e^{-\infty}) - (1 - e^{-6}) = e^{-6} = 0.002\,48.$$

> $e^{-\infty} = 0.$

The probability that the next interval is less than 1.5 s is

$$F(1.5) - F(0) = (1 - e^{-3}) - (1 - e^{0}) = 0.950.$$

> $e^{0} = 1.$

This exponential distribution will have a mean of $1/2 = 0.5$ s. Therefore the average number of cars passing the point per second is $1/0.5 = 2$.

In general the intervals between successive events, from a Poisson distribution with mean λ, are distributed according to the exponential distribution with parameter λ.

Worked example 2.1

Olan is employed by an engineering firm to watch a monitor and to give a warning when the monitor signals that action is needed to adjust a production process. The interval, X hours, between successive signals follows an exponential distribution with parameter 0.08.

(a) Find the probability that the interval between the next two signals is:
  (i) between 10 and 20 hours,
  (ii) less than two hours,
  (iii) longer than 50 hours.

(b) State the mean and standard deviation of the intervals between successive signals.

(c) Olan decides to read a newspaper for a few minutes instead of watching the monitor. How long can Olan read for if the probability of missing a signal is to be less than 0.01?

Solution

(a) The exponential distribution with parameter 0.08 has the cumulative distribution function
$$F(x) = 1 - e^{-0.08x} \qquad x > 0.$$
  (i) $P(10 < X < 20) = (1 - e^{-1.6}) - (1 - e^{-0.8})$
  $$(1 - 0.2019) - (1 - 0.4493)$$
  $$= 0.247$$
  (ii) $P(X < 2) = 1 - e^{-0.16} = 1 - 0.8521 = 0.148$
  (iii) $P(X > 50) = 1 - (1 - e^{-4}) = 0.0183$

(b) The mean of the distribution is $1/0.08 = 12.5$ hours.
The standard deviation is also equal to 12.5 hours.

(c) $P(X < k) = 1 - e^{-0.08k}$
If the probability of a signal is to be less than 0.01 then

$$0.01 = 1 - e^{-0.08k}$$
$$0.99 = e^{-0.08k}$$
$$\ln 0.99 = -0.08k$$
$$-0.01005 = -0.08k$$
$$k = 0.1256 \text{ hours}$$
$$k = 7.54 \text{ minutes}$$

Hence Olan can read his paper for about seven and a half minutes if he is prepared to take a one in a hundred chance of missing a signal.

If you are not familiar with logarithms it is possible to use trial and improvement to answer this question. You are unlikely to meet a question like **(c)** in an examination.

Worked example 2.2 _____

The probability that the lifetime, H, of a certain type of electrical component is more than h hours is given by

$$P(H > h) = e^{-h/1000} \qquad h > 0.$$

(a) Determine the probability that a randomly selected component has a lifetime of:
   (i) more than 1500 hours,
   (ii) between 1000 and 2000 hours,
   (iii) precisely 1200 hours.

(b) Calculate the probability that three components, chosen at random, all have lifetimes of more than 1500 hours.

Solution

(a) In this case H follows the exponential distribution but instead of $P(H < h)$, the cumulative probability distribution, being given, $P(H > h)$ has been given.
   (i) The probability of a lifetime more than 1500 hours is

$$e^{-1500/1000} = e^{-1.5} = 0.223.$$

   (ii) The probability of a lifetime between 1000 and 2000 hours is

$$P(H > 1000) - P(H > 2000)$$
$$= e^{-1000/1000} - e^{-2000/1000} = e^{-1} - e^{-2}$$
$$= 0.367\,88 - 0.135\,34 = 0.233$$

   (iii) Since this is a continuous distribution the probability that the lifetime is precisely 1200 hours is zero.

(b) From **(a)(i)** the probability that a randomly selected component will have a lifetime more than 1500 hours is 0.223 13. Hence the probability that three randomly selected components will all have lifetimes more than 1500 hours is

$$0.233\,13^3 = 0.0111.$$

> In this unit some examination questions will require material from earlier units. This part needs probability from S1.

EXERCISE 2A _____

1 The interval, T minutes, between successive telephone calls to a school office follows an exponential distribution with parameter 0.2. Find the probability that the interval between the next two telephone calls will be:

   (a) between 3 and 6 minutes,
   (b) between 2 and 7 minutes,
   (c) longer than 8 minutes,
   (d) less than 10 minutes.

2 The time, X days, between successive replacements of a printer cartridge may be modelled by the following distribution function.

$$P(X < x) = 1 - e^{-x/65} \qquad x > 0$$

Calculate the probability that the time between successive replacements of the cartridge is between 50 and 75 days.

3 The probability that the time, T minutes, between successive incoming calls to a telephone switchboard is less than t minutes, is given by

$$P(T < t) = 1 - e^{-t/4} \qquad t > 0.$$

Determine the probability that the time between successive incoming calls is:

(a) less than 5 minutes,

(b) between 2.5 minutes and 7.5 minutes,

(c) more than 10 minutes.

4 Large amounts of cable are produced in a factory. Faults in the cable occur at random. The distance, X m, between neighbouring faults may be modelled by an exponential distribution with parameter 0.005.

(a) Find the probability that the distance between two neighbouring faults is:
(i) less than 200 m,
(ii) between 150 m and 550 m,
(iii) between 100 m and 1000 m,
(iv) greater than 350 m,
(v) exactly 100 m.

(b) Evaluate the mean and variance of X.

5 Tubes used for street lighting in a large city have lives, in hours, which may be modelled by the random variable T with probability density function

$$f(t) = \begin{cases} 0.0002e^{-0.0002t} & t > 0 \\ 0 & \text{otherwise.} \end{cases}$$

(a) Find the probability that a randomly selected street light will last:
(i) less than 1000 hours,
(ii) between 6500 and 7500 hours,
(iii) between 3600 and 6300 hours,
(iv) more than 10 000 hours.

(b) It is decided to replace bulbs after k hours whether or not they have failed. Find k, if the probability of a bulb failing before it is replaced is to be:
(i) 0.01, **(ii)** 0.1, **(iii)** 0.3, **(iv)** 0.5.

You may find this part difficult.

(c) State the mean and standard deviation of:
   (i) T,
   (ii) the mean life of a random sample of 90 tubes.
(d) Find, approximately the probability that the mean life of a random sample of 90 tubes will be less than 5500 hours.

> You will need to use the Central Limit Theorem from S1.

6 The lives of electric light bulbs, T hours, follow an exponential distribution with cumulative distribution function

$$F(t) = \begin{cases} 1 - e^{-0.004t} & t > 0 \\ 0 & \text{otherwise.} \end{cases}$$

(a) Find the probability that a bulb will last:
   (i) between 200 and 300 hours,
   (ii) between 250 and 350 hours,
   (iii) more than 400 hours,
   (iv) less than 100 hours.

(b) State the mean and standard deviation of:
   (i) T,
   (ii) the mean life of a random sample of 225 bulbs.

> See **5(c)**.

(c) Find, approximately, the probability that the mean life of a random sample of 225 bulbs will be less than 240 hours.

7 The time taken, X minutes, by public utility company A to answer a telephone enquiry may be modelled by the following probability density function:

$$f(x) = \begin{cases} \left(\frac{1}{108}\right)x^2(6-x) & 0 < x < 6 \\ 0 & \text{elsewhere} \end{cases}$$

(a) Determine the expected time taken.
(b) Calculate the probability that a telephone enquiry is answered in less than three minutes.

The time taken, Y minutes, by public utility company B to answer a telephone enquiry has an exponential distribution with probability density function

$$g(y) = \begin{cases} \left(\frac{1}{3.6}\right)e^{\frac{-y}{3.6}} & y > 0 \\ 0 & \text{elsewhere.} \end{cases}$$

(c) Determine which of the two companies, A or B, is more likely to answer a telephone enquiry:
   (i) within 3 minutes, (ii) within 6 minutes. [A]

2.3 Fitting an exponential distribution

In chapter 6 you will study how to test whether or not the exponential distribution provides an adequate model for an observed set of data. This will require you to fit an exponential distribution to an observed frequency distribution. The data will be divided into classes and fitting an exponential distribution means calculating the expected number of observations in each class assuming that the data is a random sample from an exponential distribution.

Worked example 2.3

The intervals of time between 120 successive breakdowns of a generator used in a factory are given in the following table.

Interval, hours	0–100	100–200	200–300	300–500	500–1000
Number of intervals	16	37	36	12	19

Fit an exponential distribution to the data.

Solution

The exponential distribution has probability density function

$$f(x) = \begin{cases} \lambda e^{-\lambda x} & x > 0, \text{ where } \lambda \text{ is a constant} \\ 0 & \text{otherwise} \end{cases}$$

In order to fit an exponential distribution we need to have a value for λ. This can be estimated from the observed data by using the fact that the mean of this exponential distribution is $1/\lambda$.

The midpoints of the classes are 50, 150, 250, 400 and 750. Using a calculator the mean is found to be 286.667.

Don't forget to enter the frequencies into your calculator.

The estimated value of λ is $1/286.667 = 0.003\,488\,4$.

You need to keep more than 3 sf, for λ to obtain a final answer correct to 3 sf.

For an exponential distribution with parameter $0.003\,488\,4$
$P(X < a) = 1 - e^{-0.003\,488\,4a}$

By substituting appropriate values for a the following table can be derived:

$P(X < 100) = 0.2945 \quad P(0 < X < 100) = 0.2945$
$P(X < 200) = 0.5023 \quad P(100 < X < 200) = 0.5023 - 0.2945 = 0.2078$
$P(X < 300) = 0.6488 \quad P(200 < X < 300) = 0.6488 - 0.5023 = 0.1466$
$P(X < 500) = 0.8252 \quad P(300 < X < 500) = 0.8252 - 0.6488 = 0.1764$
$P(X > 500) = 1 - 0.8252 = 0.1748$

Since there were 120 intervals observed the numbers expected in each class is found by multiplying the probabilities by 120.

Interval, hours	0–100	100–200	200–300	300–500	>500
Number of intervals	16	37	36	12	19
Expected number of intervals	35.34	24.93	17.59	21.17	20.98

When fitting a distribution the classes should include all possible outcomes. Although the last class for the observed data was 500–1000, the last class for the fitted data should be >500. (Alternatively one additional class, >1000, with no observed values could have been included.)

Note that the expected number is the average number expected in the long run if this trial were repeated. Although the observed number must be an integer there is no reason why the expected number must be an integer.

An examination of the table shows that there is no similarity between the observed numbers and the expected numbers. Hence we can conclude that the intervals do not follow an exponential distribution.

We can further interpret this to mean that the breakdowns do not follow a Poisson distribution. That is, they do not occur at random at a constant average rate.

> Giving 2 dp for the expected numbers may seem excessive. However in chapter 6 you will use expected numbers in further calculations and will need to keep 2 dp to obtain an accurate final answer.

EXERCISE 2B

1 Fit an exponential distribution with parameter 0.25 to the following data.

Class	0–3	3–6	6–10	>10
Frequency	12	14	9	5

> In this question the parameter is given and so does not need to be estimated from the data.

2 Fit an exponential distribution to the following data.

Class	0–	5–	10–	15–	20–25
Frequency	9	13	10	5	3

> Here you need to estimate the parameter from the data.

3 During a study of booking office facilities at a railway station in a small town, the intervals of time between successive people joining a queue to buy tickets are observed. The results are summarised below.

Time interval, s	0–	50–	100–	150–	200–	300–400
Frequency	45	24	22	15	12	7

(a) Fit an exponential distribution to the data.

(b) Does the exponential distribution appear to provide an adequate model for the data? [A]

4 An old water pipeline is checked for leaks. The lengths of pipe between successive leaks is summarised below.

Distance between leaks, m	0–100	100–200	200–400	400–800	800–1500
Frequency	22	29	21	17	9

(a) Fit an exponential distribution to the data.

(b) Does the exponential distribution appear to provide an adequate model for the data?

(c) Is the data consistent with leaks occurring randomly along the pipeline? Explain your answer. [A]

5 The intervals of time between successive bicycles passing a point on a disused railway line which has been redeveloped as a cycle track were recorded.

Time interval, s	0–10	10–20	20–30	30–50	50–100	100–300
Frequency	42	12	19	16	18	13

(a) Fit an exponential distribution to the data.

(b) Give two reasons why the exponential distribution is unlikely to provide an adequate model for the data. One should be based on your calculations and the other on the scenario described. [A]

Key point summary

1 The exponential distribution has probability density function
$$f(x) = \begin{cases} \lambda e^{-\lambda x} & x > 0, \text{ where } \lambda \text{ is a constant} \\ 0 & \text{otherwise} \end{cases}$$
p 15

2 The exponential distribution with parameter λ has mean $1/\lambda$ and standard deviation $1/\lambda$.
p 15

3 $P(X < x)$ is known as the cumulative distribution function and is usually denoted $F(x)$.
p 16

4 If a and b are two constants and a > b, the probability that X takes a value between a and b is $F(a) - F(b)$.
p 16

5 For the exponential distribution with parameter λ $F(x) = 1 - e^{-\lambda x}$ $x > 0$.
p 16

6 The intervals between successive events from a Poisson distribution with mean λ are distributed according to the exponential distribution with parameter λ.
p 16

Test yourself	What to review
1 Write down the probability density function of the exponential distribution with parameter 7.	*Section 2.1*
2 Write down the cumulative distribution function of an exponential distribution with parameter 2.9.	*Section 2.2*
3 The random variable Y has probability density function $$f(y) = \begin{cases} 2.5e^{-2.5y} & y > 0 \\ 0 & \text{otherwise} \end{cases}$$ Write down the mean, standard deviation and variance of Y.	*Section 2.1*
4 X is a random variable which follows an exponential distribution with parameter 3. Find the probability that X **(a)** lies between 0.2 and 0.4, **(b)** exceeds 0.5.	*Section 2.2*

Test yourself (*continued*)	What to review

5 The random variable Y follows an exponential distribution with mean 5. Find the probability that Y

Section 2.2

   (a) is less than 4,

   (b) is exactly equal to 4.

6 The number of cars per minute passing a point on a quiet road follows a Poisson distribution with mean 0.8 per minute. Find the probability that the interval of time between two successive cars passing is longer than two minutes.

Section 2.2

Test yourself ANSWERS

1 $f(x) = \begin{cases} 7e^{-7x} & x > 0 \\ 0 & \text{otherwise.} \end{cases}$

2 $F(x) = 1 - e^{-2.9x}$ $x > 0$.

3 0.4, 0.4, 0.16.

4 **(a)** 0.248; **(b)** 0.223.

5 **(a)** 0.551; **(b)** 0.

6 0.202.

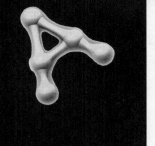

CHAPTER 3

Estimation

Learning objectives

After studying this chapter you should be able to:

■ calculate confidence intervals for the variance and the standard deviation of a normal distribution.

3.1 Introduction

In chapter 4 of S2, the idea of a confidence interval was introduced. Confidence intervals are used when we want to estimate a population parameter from a sample. The parameter may be estimated by the value of a sample statistic (point estimate) but it is usually preferable to estimate it by an interval that will give some indication of the amount of uncertainty attached to the estimate.

In chapter 2 of S4, confidence intervals for the mean of a normal population with known (z-values) and unknown (t-values) standard deviation were considered. In the latter case, the sample variance, s^2, was used as an unbiased point estimate of the population variance, σ^2.

We now consider the method for measuring the uncertainty attached to using S^2 as an estimator for σ^2.

> Note that s^2 is a particular value of the random variable S^2 (cf. $\bar{x}$ and $\bar{X}$).

3.2 Confidence intervals for a normal population variance and standard deviation

When repeated samples, each of size n, are drawn from a population, then it is almost certain that, on calculation, the result will be a set of different values for the sample mean and a set of different values for the sample variance. Hence, just as a value of the sample mean is subject to uncertainty, so is a value of the sample variance. Providing a population is normal, it is possible to estimate a population variance with a confidence interval rather than simply using a single value as a point estimate.

To do this we use the fact that if $X_1, X_2, X_3, \ldots, X_n$ denotes a random sample of size n from a normal population with variance σ^2, and S^2 denotes the sample estimate of σ^2, then

$$\frac{\sum_{i=1}^{n}(X_i - \overline{X})^2}{\sigma^2} = \frac{(n-1)S^2}{\sigma^2} \sim \chi^2_{n-1}$$

(chi-squared with $v = n - 1$ degrees of freedom).

This formula is given in the AQA booklet of formulae and tables.

Remember from chapter 5 of S4, that the χ^2-distribution is non-symmetrical over the interval 0 to ∞.

Here, as there, the **degrees of freedom** may be thought of as a measure of the number of pieces of information available for calculating the sample variance. Since variance is a measure of spread, a sample of size 1 gives no information. A sample of size 2 gives one piece of information and a sample of size 3 gives two pieces of information. In general, a sample of size n gives $n - 1$ pieces of information for the calculation of the sample variance.

From the diagram,

$$P\left(\chi^2_{n-1\left(\frac{\alpha}{2}\right)} < \chi^2_{n-1} < \chi^2_{n-1\left(1-\frac{\alpha}{2}\right)}\right) = 100(1-\alpha)\%.$$

Hence,

$$P\left(\chi^2_{n-1\left(\frac{\alpha}{2}\right)} < \frac{(n-1)S^2}{\sigma^2} < \chi^2_{n-1\left(1-\frac{\alpha}{2}\right)}\right) = 100(1-\alpha)\%.$$

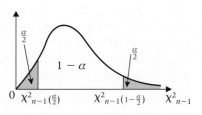

Rearrangement of this gives,

$$P\left(\frac{(n-1)S^2}{\chi^2_{n-1\left(1-\frac{\alpha}{2}\right)}} < \sigma^2 < \frac{(n-1)S^2}{\chi^2_{n-1\left(\frac{\alpha}{2}\right)}}\right) = 100(1-\alpha)\%.$$

Note that when using the AQA booklet of formulae and tables $p = 1 - \frac{\alpha}{2}$.

Thus the $100(1 - \alpha)\%$ confidence interval for a normal population variance, σ^2, is given by the following limits:

$$\frac{(n-1)s^2}{\chi^2_{n-1\left(1-\frac{\alpha}{2}\right)}} \quad \text{and} \quad \frac{(n-1)s^2}{\chi^2_{n-1\left(\frac{\alpha}{2}\right)}}$$

Note that although σ^2 is unknown, it does not vary. It is the intervals that vary from sample to sample.

A confidence interval for a normal population standard deviation, σ, is obtained by simply taking the square root of each of these limits.

Remember that, whilst the variance has useful mathematical properties, the standard deviation is the natural measure of spread. Hence confidence limits for both are useful.

Worked example 3.1

The time a bus takes to travel from Chorlton to All Saints during the morning rush hour may be assumed to be normally distributed. A random sample of six journeys took 23, 19, 25, 34, 24 and 28 minutes.

Find:

(a) a 95% confidence interval,

(b) a 99% confidence interval,

for the standard deviation of journey time.

Solution

Using a calculator

$$s = 5.089\,20, \; s^2 = 25.9, \; (n-1)s^2 = 5 \times 25.9 = 129.5$$

(a) The upper and lower 0.025 tails will result in a probability of 0.95 (95%) between them.

Thus from Table 6 with $v = n - 1 = 5$,
lower value $(0.025) = 0.831$
upper value $(0.975) = 12.833$

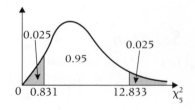

Thus a 95% confidence interval for the variance of journey time is given by

$$\frac{129.5}{12.833} \quad \text{and} \quad \frac{129.5}{0.831},$$

i.e.

$$(10.09, \; 155.84) \text{ minutes}^2.$$

Hence, a 95% confidence interval for the standard deviation of journey time is given by

$$\sqrt{10.09} \quad \text{and} \quad \sqrt{155.84},$$

i.e.

$$(3.2, \; 12.5) \text{ minutes}.$$

(b) For a 99% confidence interval,
lower value $(0.005) = 0.412$
upper value $(0.995) = 16.750$
These then give a 99% confidence interval for the standard deviation of journey time as

$$\sqrt{\frac{129.5}{16.750}} \quad \text{and} \quad \sqrt{\frac{129.5}{0.412}},$$

i.e.

$$(2.8, \; 17.7) \text{ minutes}.$$

Note that:
- The value of s (5.1) lies within the interval as clearly it always must!
- The interval is **not** symmetrical about s.

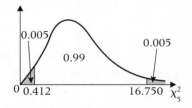

Note that the higher the confidence, the wider the interval.

3

Worked example 3.2

In processing grain in the brewing industry, the percentage extract recovered is measured. A particular brewery introduces a new source of grain and the percentage extract on 11 separate days is as follows.

95.2 93.1 93.5 95.9 94.0 92.0 94.4 93.2 95.5 92.3 95.4

(a) Regarding the sample as a random sample from a normal population, calculate:

   (i) a 90% confidence interval for the population variance,

   (ii) a 90% confidence interval for the population mean.

(b) The previous source of grain gave daily percentage extract figures that were normally distributed with mean 94.2 and standard deviation 2.5. A high percentage extract is desirable but the brewery manager also requires as little day-to-day variation as possible. Without further calculation, compare the two sources of grain. [A]

Solution

(a) From a calculator $\bar{x} = 94.045$ and $s = 1.341\,17$.

   (i) From Table 6 with $v = n - 1 = 10$,
      lower value (0.05) = 3.940
      upper value (0.95) = 18.307

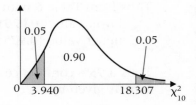

A 90% confidence interval for the population variance is given by

$$\frac{10 \times 1.341\,17^2}{18.307} \quad \text{and} \quad \frac{10 \times 1.341\,17^2}{3.940},$$

i.e.

(0.98, 4.57).

   (ii) A confidence interval for a population mean, σ unknown, is of the form

$$\bar{x} \pm t_{n-1} \times \frac{s}{\sqrt{n}}.$$

Refer to section 2.4 of S4.

From Table 5, $t_{10(0.95)} = 1.812$.

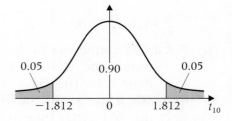

Thus, a 90% confidence interval for the population mean is given by

$$94.045 \pm 1.812 \times \frac{1.341\,17}{\sqrt{11}},$$

i.e.

(93.3, 94.8).

(b) The mean for the previous source of grain was 94.2. This lies well within the confidence interval calculated for the mean of the new source of grain. Therefore there is no evidence that the means differ.

The standard deviation for the previous source of grain was 2.5 and so the variance was $2.5^2 = 6.25$. This is above the upper limit of the confidence interval for the variance of the new source of grain. This suggests that the new source of grain has less variability.

Combining these two conclusions suggests that the new source of grain is preferable to the previous source.

EXERCISE 3A

1 Samples of a high temperature lubricant were tested and the temperatures ($^\circ$C) at which they ceased to be effective were as follows:

235 242 235 240 237 234 239 237

Assuming temperature to be normally distributed, determine a 95% confidence interval for the population variance.

2 In a study aimed at improving the design of bus cabs, the functional arm reach of a random sample of bus drivers was measured. The results, in millimetres, were as follows:

701 642 651 700 672 674 656 649

Given that functional arm reach may be assumed to be normally distributed, determine a 90% confidence interval for the population standard deviation.

3 As part of a research study on pattern recognition, a random sample of students on a design course was asked to examine a picture and see if they could recognise a word. The picture contained the word *technology* written backwards. The times, in seconds, taken to recognise the word were as follows:

55 28 79 54 87 61 62 68 38

Calculate:

(a) a 95% confidence interval for the variance,

(b) a 99% confidence interval for the variance.

Assume recognition time to be normally distributed.

4 The external diameters, in centimetres, of a random sample of piston rings produced on a particular machine were

9.91 9.89 10.12 9.98 10.09 9.81 10.01 9.99 9.86.

Calculate a 95% confidence interval for the standard deviation. You may assume external diameters to be normally distributed. Do your results support the manufacturer's claim that the standard deviation is 0.06 cm?

5 The vitamin C content of a random sample of five lemons was measured. The results in 'mg per 10 g' were

   1.04 0.95 0.63 1.62 1.11.

Assuming a normal distribution, calculate a 95% confidence interval for the standard deviation.

A greengrocer claimed that the method of determining the vitamin C content was extremely unreliable and that the observed variability was due more to errors in the determination rather than to actual differences between lemons. To check this, seven independent determinations were made of the vitamin C content of the same lemon. The results were as follows:

   1.21 1.22 1.21 1.23 1.24 1.23 1.22

Assuming a normal distribution, calculate a 90% confidence interval for the standard deviation of the determinations. Does your result support the greengrocer's claim?

6 A car insurance company found that the average amount it was paying on bodywork claims was £435 with a standard deviation of £141. The next eight bodywork claims were subjected to extra investigation before payment was agreed. The payments, in pounds, on these claims were

   48 109 237 192 403 98 264 68.

(a) Assuming these data can be regarded as a random sample from a normal distribution, calculate a 90% confidence interval for:
   (i) the mean payment after extra investigation,
   (ii) the standard deviation of the payments after extra investigation.

(b) Explain to the manager whether or not your results suggest that the distribution of payments has changed after special investigation, and comment on her suggestion that in future all claims over £900 should be subject to special investigation. [A]

7 As part of an investigation into the quality of hot dog sausages, the fat content, x per cent, of each sausage in a random sample of ten hot dogs was measured with the results as follows:

   25.2 21.3 22.8 17.0 29.8 21.0 25.5 16.0 20.9 19.5

(a) Assuming percentage fat content to be normally distributed, calculate a 95% confidence interval for the variance of the fat content of hot dog sausages.

(b) State, giving a reason, whether or not you would agree with the claim that the standard deviation of the fat content of hot dog sausages is less than five per cent.
[A]

8 The resistances (in ohms) of a sample from a batch of resistors were

    2314 2456 2389 2361 2360 2332 2402.

Assume that the sample is from a normal distribution.

(a) Calculate a 90% confidence interval for the standard deviation of the batch.

Past experience suggests that the standard deviation, σ, is 35 Ω.

(b) Calculate a 95% confidence interval for the mean resistance of the batch:
    (i) assuming $\sigma = 35$,
    (ii) making no assumption about the standard deviation.

(c) Compare the merits of the confidence intervals calculated in **(b)**.   [A]

9 A car manufacturer introduces a new method of assembling a component. The old method had a mean assembly time of 42 minutes with a standard deviation of 4 minutes. The manufacturer would like the assembly time to be as short as possible and to have as little variation as possible. He expects the new method to have a smaller mean but to leave the variability unchanged. A random sample of assembly times, in minutes, taken after the new method had become established was

    27 19 68 41 17 52 35 72 38.

A statistician glanced at the data and said she thought the variability had increased.

(a) Suggest why she said this.

(b) Assuming the data may be regarded as a random sample from a normal distribution, calculate a 95% confidence interval for the standard deviation. Does this confirm the statistician's claim or not?

(c) Calculate a 90% confidence interval for the mean using a method which is appropriate in the light of your answer to **(b)**.

(d) Comment on the suitability of the new process.   [A]

10 Stud anchors are used in the construction industry. Samples are tested by embedding them in concrete and applying a steadily increasing load until the stud fails.

(a) A sample of six tests gave the following maximum loads in kN:

    27.0 30.5 28.0 23.0 27.5 26.5

Assuming a normal distribution for maximum loads, find 95% confidence intervals for:

(i) the mean,

(ii) the standard deviation.

(b) If the mean was at the lower end and the standard deviation at the upper end of the confidence intervals calculated in **(a)**, find the value of k which the maximum load would exceed with probability 0.99.

Safety regulations state that the greatest load that may be applied under working conditions is $\dfrac{(\bar{x} - 2s)}{3}$, where $\bar{x}$ is the mean and s^2 is the unbiased estimate of variance calculated from a sample of six tests. Calculate this figure for the data above and comment on the adequacy of this regulation in these circumstances.

[A]

Key point summary

1 If S^2 denotes the variance estimate from a random sample of size n from a normal population with variance σ^2, then

p 26

$$\frac{(n-1)S^2}{\sigma^2} \sim \chi^2_{n-1}.$$

2 The χ^2-distribution is not symmetric so both lower and upper percentage points need to be read from tables.

p 26

3 A $100(1 - \alpha)\%$ confidence interval for a normal population variance, σ^2, is given by

p 26

$$\frac{(n-1)s^2}{\chi^2_{n-1\left(1-\frac{\alpha}{2}\right)}} \quad \text{and} \quad \frac{(n-1)s^2}{\chi^2_{n-1\left(\frac{\alpha}{2}\right)}}.$$

4 Confidence limits for a normal population standard deviation, σ, are found by taking the square root of those calculated for the population variance.

p 26

Test yourself

What to review

1 Find the upper and lower 2.5 percentage points for a χ^2 distribution having 20 degrees of freedom.

Section 3.2

2 The times, in seconds, taken by a random sample of 12 six-year-old children to complete a simple task were as follows:

23 32 18 26 30 35 20 29 21 33 25 20

Assuming times to be normally distributed, determine a 90% confidence interval for the population variance.

Section 3.2

Test yourself (*continued*)	**What to review**

3 The sausage content, x g, in each of a random sample of 25 sausage rolls made by a local butcher was determined. Computations resulted in a value of 23 for s, the sample standard deviation estimate.

Section 3.2

Assuming sausage content to be normally distributed with variance σ^2, construct a 99% confidence interval for σ. Hence, comment on the claim that $\sigma < 28$.

4 The moisture content, x per cent, of each of a random sample of 15 batches of a particular chemical was determined. Subsequent calculations resulted in

Section 3.2

$$S_{xx} = 61.74.$$

Given that moisture content may be assumed to be normally distributed, determine a 95% confidence interval for the standard deviation of moisture content in all such batches of the chemical.

5 It is known that repeated weighings of the same object on a particular chemical balance give readings which are normally distributed with mean equal to the mass of the object. Past experience suggests that the standard deviation, σ, is 0.25 mg. Seven repeated weighings gave the following readings (mg):

Section 3.2

19.3 19.5 19.1 19.0 19.8 19.7 19.4

(a) Use these data to calculate a 95% confidence interval for σ.

(b) Calculate a 95% confidence interval for the mass of the object assuming $\sigma = 0.25$ mg.

(c) Calculate a 95% confidence interval for the mass of the object, making no assumption about σ, and using only data from the sample.

(d) Give **two** reasons for preferring the confidence interval calculated in **(b)** to that calculated in **(c)**.

Test yourself ANSWERS

1 9.591 and 34.170.

2 (18.4–79.1).

3 (16.7–35.8),
Reject claim that $\sigma < 28$ as upper limit is greater than 28.

4 (1.54–3.31).

5 (a) (0.19–0.65); **(b)** (19.21–19.59); **(c)** (19.13–19.67);
(d) Past experience suggests $\sigma = 0.25$ and this is consistent with current sample (0.25 within confidence interval in **(a)**).
Using 'known' value of σ leads to narrower confidence interval.

CHAPTER 4

Hypothesis testing: one-sample tests

Learning objectives

After studying this chapter you should be able to:

- carry out a test for a normal population variance
- test hypotheses for a binomial population proportion, either by calculating exact probabilities or by using an appropriate approximation
- test hypotheses for the mean of a Poisson population parameter, either by calculating exact probabilities or by using a normal approximation.

4.1 Introduction

In chapter 2 of S3 and chapter 3 of S4 you were introduced to some important basic concepts of hypothesis testing:

Null hypothesis (H_0):	an assertion that a parameter in a statistical model takes a particular value, and is assumed true until experimental evidence suggests otherwise.
Alternative hypothesis (H_1):	expresses the way in which the value of a parameter may deviate from that specified in the null hypothesis, and is assumed true when the experimental evidence suggests that the null hypothesis is false.
Type 1 error:	rejecting the null hypothesis when it is, in fact, true.
Type 2 error:	accepting the null hypothesis when it is, in fact, false.
Test statistic:	a function of a sample of observations which provides a basis for testing the validity of the null hypothesis.
Critical region:	the null hypothesis is rejected when a calculated value of the test statistic lies within this region.
Critical value:	the value which determines the boundary of the critical region.

Significance level (α):   the size of the critical region; the probability of a Type 1 error.

One-tailed test: the critical region is located wholly at one end of the sampling distribution of the test statistic; H_1 involves < or > but not both.

Two-tailed test: the critical region comprises areas at both ends of the sampling distribution of the test statistic; H_1 involves $\neq$.

As a reminder of how these concepts are applied, let us consider a *t*-test for a population mean μ.

Worked example 4.1

A consumer group, concerned about the mean fat content of a certain grade of steakburger, submits a random sample of 12 steakburgers to an independent laboratory for analysis. The percentage of fat in each of the steakburgers is as follows:

21 18 19 16 18 24 22 19 24 14 18 15

The manufacturer claims that the mean fat content of this grade of steakburger is less than 20%. Assuming percentage fat content to be normally distributed, carry out an appropriate hypothesis test in order to advise the consumer group as to the validity of the manufacturer's claim.

Solution

You will recall that from Section 4.2 of S4 that if

$$X \sim N(\mu, \sigma^2)$$

then

$$\frac{\overline{X} - \mu}{\frac{S}{\sqrt{n}}} \sim t_{n-1}$$

> This formula is given in the AQA booklet of formulae and tables.

where $\overline{X} = \dfrac{1}{n}\sum X$

and $S^2 = \dfrac{\sum (X - \bar{X})^2}{n - 1}$.

H_0: $\mu = 20\%$
H_1: $\mu < 20\%$ (one-tailed)
Significance level, $\alpha = 0.05$ (say)
Degrees of freedom, $v = n - 1 = 11$
Critical region, $t < -1.796$

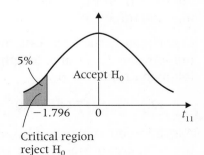

5%

Accept H_0

-1.796 0 t_{11}

Critical region
reject H_0

Under H_0, $\overline{X} \sim N\left(20, \dfrac{\sigma^2}{12}\right)$

Now the test statistic is

$$t = \frac{\bar{x} - \mu}{\frac{s}{\sqrt{n}}}$$

with $\bar{x} = 19$ and $s = 3.247$.

Hence, $t = \dfrac{19 - 20}{\dfrac{3.247}{\sqrt{12}}} = -1.07$.

This value does not lie in the critical region. Thus there is no evidence, at the 5% level of significance, to support the manufacturer's claim.

4.2 Normal population variance

From section 3.2 we have seen that if $X_1, X_2, X_3, \ldots, X_n$ denotes a random sample of size n from a normal population with variance σ^2, and S^2 denotes the estimate of σ^2 made from the sample, then

$$\frac{\sum_{i=1}^{n} (X_i - \overline{X})^2}{\sigma^2} = \frac{(n-1)\,S^2}{\sigma^2} \sim \chi^2_{n-1}$$

(chi-squared with $v = n - 1$ degrees of freedom).

This formula is given in the AQA booklet of formulae and tables.

The statistic $\dfrac{(n-1)\,s^2}{\sigma^2}$ may thus be used to test hypotheses concerning a normal population variance or, by implication, a normal population standard deviation.

Worked example 4.2

A user of a certain gauge of steel wire suspects that the standard deviation of its breaking strength, in newtons (N), is different from the value of 0.75 as specified by the manufacturer.

Consequently the user tests the breaking strength of each of a random sample of nine lengths of wire and obtains the following results:

    72.1   74.5   72.8   75.0   73.4   75.4   76.1   73.5   74.1

Assuming breaking strength to be normally distributed, test, at the 10% level of significance, the manufacturer's specification.

Solution

H_0: $\sigma = 0.75\,\text{N}$ or H_0: $\sigma^2 = 0.5625\,\text{N}^2$

H_1: $\sigma \neq 0.75\,\text{N}$ or H_1: $\sigma^2 \neq 0.5625\,\text{N}^2$ (two-tailed)

Significance level, $\alpha = 0.10$

Degrees of freedom, $\nu = 8$

Critical region, $\chi^2 < 2.733$ or $\chi^2 > 15.507$

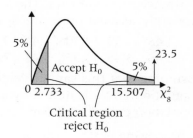

From your calculator,

$$(n-1)s^2 = 8 \times 1.284\,52^2$$
$$= 13.2$$

Under H_0, $\chi^2 = \dfrac{(n-1)s^2}{\sigma^2} = \dfrac{13.2}{0.5625} = 23.5$

This value does lie in the critical region. Thus there is evidence, at the 10% level of significance, to dispute the manufacturer's specification as regards variability of breaking strength.

EXERCISE 4A

1 During a particular week, 13 babies were born in a maternity unit. Part of the standard procedure is to measure the length of the baby. Given below is a list of the lengths, in centimetres, of the babies born in this particular week.

  49 50 45 51 47 49 48 54 53 55 45 50 48

Assuming that this sample came from an underlying normal population, test, at the 5% significance level, the hypothesis that the population standard deviation of length is 2.5 cm.

[A]

2 A random sample of 12 steel ingots was taken from a production line. The masses, in kilograms, of these ingots are given below.

  24.8 30.8 28.1 24.8 27.4 22.1
  24.7 27.3 27.5 27.8 23.9 23.2

Assuming that this sample came from an underlying normal population, investigate the claim that the population standard deviation is greater than 2 kg.

[A]

3 A random sample of 14 cows was selected from a large dairy herd at Brookfield Farm. The milk yield in one week was recorded, in kilograms, for each cow. The results are given below.

  169.6 142.0 103.3 111.6 123.4 143.5 155.1
  101.7 170.7 113.2 130.9 146.1 169.3 155.5

Stating clearly any distributional assumptions that you make, test the hypothesis that the standard deviation of yield for the herd at Brookfield Farm is 20 kg.

[A]

4 The variability in unit mass is very critical in the pharmaceutical industry. The mass, in grams, of each of 15 randomly selected units of a specific drug is as follows:

>3.48   3.52   3.50   3.47   3.49   3.54   3.51   3.52
>3.46   3.45   3.55   3.48   3.51   3.52   3.50

Assuming that this sample comes from an underlying normal population, investigate the hypothesis that the variance of the population exceeds $0.002\,\text{g}^2$. [A]

5 In processing grain in the brewing industry, the percentage extract recovered is measured. A particular brewer introduces a new source of grain and the percentage extract on 11 separate days is as follows:

>95.2   93.1   93.5   95.9   94.0   92.0
>94.4   93.2   95.5   92.3   95.4

Prior to introducing the new source of grain, the variance of percentage extract recovered was 6.0. Does the new source of grain result in a decrease in the variability of percentage extract recovered? What assumptions have you made in carrying out your test? [A]

6 A car manufacturer introduces a new method of assembling a particular component. A random sample of assembly times (minutes), taken after the new method has become established, is

>27   39   28   41   47   42   35   32   38.

The old assembly method had a standard deviation of eight minutes and the manufacturer assumes the new method of assembly will reduce this value. Assuming assembly times to be normally distributed, investigate the manufacturer's assumption. [A]

4.3 Binomial population proportion

In situations where the population parameter of interest in a hypothesis test is a proportion, or percentage, rather than a mean or variance, then a binomial distribution, or an appropriate approximation, provides the basis for the test.

Remember from chapter 5 of S1 that if X denotes the number of successes in n repeated trials, each of which may result in a success with probability p,

then	$X \sim \text{B}(n, p)$
and	$P(X = x) = \binom{n}{x} p^x (1-p)^{n-x} \quad x = 0, 1, 2, \ldots, n$
where	$\binom{n}{x} = \dfrac{n!}{x!(n-x)!}$

Worked example 4.3

Until recently, an average of 60 out of every 100 patients have survived a particularly severe infection. When a new drug is administered to a random sample of 15 patients with the infection, 12 survive. Does this provide evidence that the new drug is effective?

Solution

Let X denote the number of patients who survive.

Then $X \sim B(15, p)$, and it is required to test

$\quad$ H_0: $p = 0.6$ $\quad$ (not effective)

$\quad$ H_1: $p > 0.6$ $\quad$ (effective; one-tailed)

Now assuming H_0 is true, $X \sim B(15, 0.6)$, and so

$$P(X = 12) = \binom{15}{12} 0.6^{12} 0.4^3 = 0.063\,39$$

$$P(X = 13) = \binom{15}{13} 0.6^{13} 0.4^2 = 0.021\,94$$

$$P(X = 14) = \binom{15}{14} 0.6^{14} 0.4^1 = 0.004\,70$$

$$P(X = 15) = \binom{15}{15} 0.6^{15} 0.4^0 = 0.000\,47$$

Hence, under H_0, the probability of

15 patients surviving	$= 0.000\,47$
14 or 15 patients surviving	$= 0.005\,17$
13, 14 or 15 patients surviving	$= 0.027\,11$
12, 13, 14 or 15 patients surviving	$= 0.090\,50$

Note that if 14 surviving is adopted as a 'significant' result, the probability of 15 must be included as well (because 15 is actually a 'better' result than 14). Similarly with 13, the probabilities for 14 or 15 must be included, and so on.

From the above (cumulative) probabilities it can be seen that the critical region for, say, a 5% test is $X \geqslant 13$

since $\quad$ $P(X \geqslant 13) = 0.027\,11 < 0.05$

but $\quad$ $P(X \geqslant 12) = 0.090\,50 > 0.05$.

The number of patients who actually survived was 12. This value does not lie in the critical region. Thus there is no evidence, at the 5% level of significance, to suggest that the drug is effective.

Note that rather than actually determine the critical region, it is equally valid to simply argue that since

$P(X \geqslant 12) = 0.090\,50 > 0.05$, then H_0 cannot be rejected.

Remember also that tables of the Cumulative Binomial Distribution Function may often provide an easier and quicker alternative for calculating probabilities or finding critical regions.

> Available in the AQA booklet of formulae and tables.

Thus, $P(X \geqslant 12 | n = 15, p = 0.6)$ is equal to

$P(X \leqslant 3 | n = 15, p = 0.4)$

which, from the tables, is equal to 0.0905, as above.

Worked example 4.4

A machine, which manufactures black polythene dustbin bags, is known to produce 3% defective bags. Following a major breakdown of the machine, extensive repair work is carried out which may result in a change in the percentage of defective bags produced. To investigate this possibility, a random sample of 200 bags is taken from the machine's production and a count reveals 12 defective bags. What may be concluded?

Solution

Here $n = 200$, $p = $ population proportion of defective bags produced, and it is required to test

> $H_0: p = 0.03$ (no change)
> $H_1: p \neq 0.03$ (change: two-tailed)
> Significance level, $\alpha = 0.05$ (say)

From section 3.2 of S2, a Poisson distribution with $\lambda = np$ provides an approximation to a binomial distribution when $n \geqslant 50$ and $p < 0.1$ (or $p > 0.9$).

Thus if X denotes the number of defective bags in the sample, then under H_0

$X \sim \text{Po}(\lambda = 200 \times 0.03 = 6.0)$

Using tables of the Cumulative Poisson Distribution Function

$P(X \geqslant 12) = 1 - P(X \leqslant 11)$
$= 1 - 0.9799 = 0.0201$

> Available in the AQA booklet of formulae and tables.

Since the test is two-tailed, this probability is compared with $\dfrac{\alpha}{2} = 0.025$, because a small number of defective bags could also lead to the rejection of the null hypothesis.

Here, $0.0201 < 0.025$ so H_0 is rejected. There is evidence, at the 5% level of significance, that the percentage of defective bags produced has changed following the repair work.

Worked example 4.5

Company *A* proposes the takeover of Company *B*. The latter's Chief Executive claims that her company's shareholders are equally divided for and against the takeover on the basis of the terms offered. However, the Chairman of Company *A* claims that more than half of Company *B*'s shareholders are in favour of accepting his company's offer.

To investigate these two rival claims, the view of each of 400 randomly selected shareholders of Company *B* is sought. A subsequent count reveals that 219 are in favour of the offer; the remainder are against.

Does this provide evidence, at the 1% significance level, that the claim made by Company *B*'s Chairman is valid?

Solution

Let *p* denote the actual proportion of Company *B*'s shareholders who are in favour of the offer. Then

H_0: $p = 0.50$ (claim of Company *B*'s Chief Executive)

H_1: $p > 0.50$ (claim of Company *A*'s Chairman; one-tailed)

Significance level, $\alpha = 0.01$

If *X* denotes the number of Company *B*'s shareholders in the sample who are in favour of the offer, then under H_0

$X \sim B(400, 0.50)$ with mean, $np = 200$ and

variance, $np(1 - p) = 100$

From section 3.3 of S2, a normal distribution provides an approximation to a binomial distribution when $n \geqslant 50$ and np is at least 10.

Thus under H_0, $X \sim N(200, 100)$, or denoting the sample proportion by $\hat{P} = \dfrac{X}{n}$ then

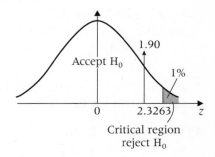

1.90

Accept H_0

1%

0   2.3263   z

Critical region reject H_0

$$\hat{P} \sim N\left(\frac{200}{400}, \frac{100}{400^2}\right)$$

i.e. $\hat{P} \sim N(0.50, 0.000\,625)$

So   Critical region, $z > 2.3263$

Now the value of sample proportion,

$$\hat{p} = \frac{219}{400} = 0.5475$$

so the test statistic,

$$z = \frac{0.5475 - 0.50}{\sqrt{0.000\,625}} = 1.90$$

> It is possible to include a continuity correction. This would give a slightly different z-value but is not required in this unit.

This value does not lie in the critical region. Thus there is no evidence, at the 1% level of significance, to support the claim of Company A's Chairman.

To test hypotheses about a binomial population proportion, p, either:

(a) determine the cumulative binomial probability of B(n, p), or

(b) determine the cumulative Poisson probability of Po$(\lambda = np)$ when $n \geqslant 50$, $p < 0.1$ (or $p > 0.9$), or

(c) use

$$\frac{\hat{P} - p}{\sqrt{\dfrac{p(1 - p)}{n}}} \sim N(0, 1)$$

when $n \geqslant 50$ and $np \geqslant 10$.

EXERCISE 4B

1 A pharmacist claims that more than 60% of all customers simply collect a prescription. One of her assistants notes that, in a random sample of 12 customers, 10 simply collected a prescription. Does this provide sufficient evidence, at the 5% level, to support the pharmacist's claim?

2 In a survey carried out in Funville, 14 children out of a random sample of 30 said that they bought the Bopper comic regularly. Test, at the 10% level of significance, the hypothesis that the true proportion of all children who buy this comic regularly is 0.35. [A]

3 Thirty randomly selected coffee drinkers were each asked to taste-test a new brand of coffee. The responses are listed below with L representing 'like', I representing 'indifferent', and D representing 'dislike'.

    L D L L D L L L L I L L L I L
    D L I L L I L L L D L L L L I

Do these data support the claim that more than half of all coffee drinkers like this new brand of coffee?

4 Tins of baked beans are packed in boxes of 24. Results from a random sample of 25 boxes delivered to supermarkets show that a total of eight tins were damaged. Assess the claim that less than 2% of tins are damaged during delivery. [A]

5 A survey of Aldervale revealed that 223 houses out of a random sample of 500 were fitted with some form of double glazing. Test the hypothesis that 40% of all houses in Aldervale have some form of double glazing. [A]

6 Prior to joining a coaching course, a netball player has scored with 45% of her shots at the basket, and so is considered to have a scoring ability of 0.45. In games following the course, she scores with 72 of her 135 shots at the basket. Stating clearly any assumptions made, investigate whether or not the course has improved her shooting ability.

4.4 Poisson population mean

In the previous section it was seen how a Poisson distribution may be used as an approximation to a binomial situation when testing hypotheses concerning a population proportion. However, there are situations for which a Poisson distribution is appropriate in its own right when testing hypotheses concerning a population mean value.

You will recall from chapter 6 of S1, that if $X \sim \mathrm{Po}(\lambda)$ then

$$P(X = x) = e^{-\lambda}\frac{\lambda^x}{x!} \quad x = 0, 1, 2, 3, \ldots,$$

with mean $= \lambda$ and variance $= \lambda$.

Available in the AQA booklet of formulae and tables.

Worked example 4.6

The number of faults in one metre of a particular type of thread is known to have a Poisson distribution. It is claimed that the average number of faults is 0.02 per metre. A random sample of 100 one metre lengths of the thread reveals a total of six faults. Does this information support the claim?

Solution

Remembering that if $A \sim \mathrm{Po}(a)$ independent of $B \sim \mathrm{Po}(b)$ then $C = A + B \sim \mathrm{Po}(a + b)$, and denoting the total number of faults in the 100 one metre lengths by X, then if the claim is valid

$X \sim \mathrm{Po}(100 \times 0.02 = 2)$.

It is thus required to test

$H_0: \lambda = 2$

$H_1: \lambda \neq 2$ (two-tailed)

Significance level, $\alpha = 0.05$ (say)

The observed number of faults is 6, and using tables of the Cumulative Poisson Distribution Function with $\lambda = 2$

Available in the AQA booklet of formulae and tables.

$P(X \geq 6) = 1 - P(X \leq 5)$

$\qquad = 1 - 0.9834 = 0.0166 < 0.025$ (two-tailed)

There is evidence, at the 5% level of significance, that the claim is not valid.

Worked example 4.7

Prior to extensive modernisation of its forecourt, the average number of vehicles calling for fuel at a small garage has been 5 per hour. Following the modernisation, a total of 543 vehicles called for fuel in a random sample of 100 one-hour intervals. Has the modernisation of the garage's forecourt significantly increased the average number of vehicles calling for fuel?

To answer this question you need to assume that vehicles arrive independently at random, and so the numbers arriving follow a Poisson distribution.

Solution

If X denotes the total number of vehicles calling for fuel in the 100 one-hour intervals, then under the null hypothesis of no increase

$$X \sim \text{Po}(100 \times 5 = 500)$$

For a Poisson distribution with a mean greater than 10, a normal distribution with $\mu = \sigma^2 = \lambda$ provides a good approximation (see section 3.4 of S2).

Hence, $X = \text{N}(500, 500)$.

The test is thus as follows.

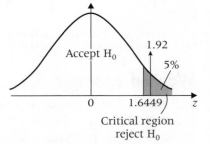

Critical region
reject H_0

H_0: $\lambda = 500$
H_1: $\lambda > 500$ (one-tailed)
Significance level, $\alpha = 0.05$ (say)
Critical region, $z > 1.6449$
Test statistic, $z = \dfrac{543 - 500}{\sqrt{500}} = 1.92$

This value does lie in the critical region. Thus there is evidence, at the 5% level of significance, to suggest that the forecourt modernisation has resulted in an increase in the average number of vehicles calling for fuel.

A continuity correction would give a slightly different z-value but is not required in this unit.

To test hypotheses about a Poisson population mean λ, either

(a)   determine the cumulative Poisson probability of $\text{Po}(\lambda)$, or

(b)   use

$$\frac{\hat{\lambda} - \lambda}{\sqrt{\lambda}} \sim \text{N}(0, 1)$$

when $\lambda > 10$.

EXERCISE 4C

1 It is known that the numbers of parasites on fish in a pond follow a Poisson distribution. The total number of parasites on a random sample of three fish taken from the pond is eight. Test the hypothesis that the mean number of parasites per fish is four.   [A]

2 In the manufacture of commercial carpet on a particular machine, small faults occur at random in the carpet at an average rate of 0.925 per 25 m². Following an overhaul of the machine, an inspection of a random sample of four 5 m × 5 m squares of carpet reveals only two small faults. Is there evidence, at the 5% level of significance, that, following the overhaul, the mean number of small faults has been reduced?

3 The daily number of letters of complaint from customers received by a department store follows a Poisson distribution. Over a 150-day period, a total of 407 letters of complaint were received. Investigate, at the 1% level of significance, the claim that an average of fewer than three letters of complaint per day are received.   [A]

4 It has been established over a period of time that the weekly numbers of breakages of crockery and glassware in a hotel follow a Poisson distribution with mean 27. On appointment, a new manager announces to staff that unless this mean level is reduced, bonuses will suffer. Following this announcement, the weekly numbers of breakages over an eight-week period were as follows.

    23   19   17   20   25   32   22   26

Do these data provide evidence that the manager's announcement has been heeded by the staff?

5 The number of faults in a 100 m roll of barbed wire may be assumed to have a Poisson distribution with mean λ. Given that a total of nine faults is found on five such rolls, investigate the claim that $\lambda < 2.8$.

6 Brindle bricks, used in laying paths and drives, are delivered on pallets each containing 400 bricks. The number of defective bricks per pallet may be modelled adequately by a Poisson distribution. The manufacturer claims that the mean number of defective bricks per pallet is equal to five. Eighteen pallets of brindle bricks are delivered to a particular address and, during the laying of these bricks, 73 are found to be defective.

(a) Test, at the 5% level of significance, the manufacturer's claim.

(b) What assumption have you made about the eighteen pallets of bricks?   [A]

MIXED EXERCISE

1 An investigation was conducted into the dust content in the flue gases of a particular type of solid-fuel boiler. Thirteen boilers were used under identical fuelling and extraction conditions. Over a similar period, the following quantities, in grams, of dust were deposited in traps inserted in each of the thirteen flues.

> 73.1 56.4 82.1 67.2 78.7 75.1 48.0
> 53.3 55.5 61.5 60.6 55.2 63.1

Stating any necessary distributional assumptions, test, at the 5% level of significance, the hypothesis that:

(a) the population variance of dust deposit is $35 \, g^2$,

(b) the population mean dust deposit is $60 \, g$. [A]

2 Smallwoods Ltd run a weekly football pools competition. One part of this involves a fixed-odds contest where the entrant has to forecast correctly the result of each of five given matches. In the event of a fully correct forecast the entrant is paid out at odds of 100 to 1. During the last two years Miss Fortune has entered this fixed-odds contest 80 times. The table below summarises her results.

Number of matches correctly forecast per entry (x)	0	1	2	3	4	5
Number of entries with x correct forecasts (f)	4	13	27	22	13	1

Assuming that the number of matches correctly forecast per entry follows a binomial distribution, test the hypothesis that the probability of Miss Fortune forecasting correctly the result of a single match is 0.5.

On the evidence before you, and assuming that the point of entering is to win money, would you advise Miss Fortune to continue with this competition, and why? [A]

3 A random sample of 15 workers from a vacuum flask assembly line was selected from a large number of such workers. Ivor Stopwatch, a work-study engineer, asked each of these workers to assemble a one-litre vacuum flask at their normal working speed. The times taken, in seconds, to complete these tasks are given below.

> 109.2 146.2 127.9   92.0 108.5   91.1 109.8 114.9
> 115.3   99.0 112.8 130.7 141.7 122.6 119.9

Assuming that this sample came from an underlying normal population, investigate the claim that the population standard deviation of assembly time is 12 s.

4 At a nuclear power station great care is taken to monitor employees' state of health. The table below gives the number of visits made by each of 10 employees from the reactor room to their general practitioners during one calendar year.

> 3 6 5 7 4 2 3 5 1 4

The number of such visits made by a member of the general public is known to have a Poisson distribution with mean 3. Assuming that the numbers of visits made by the nuclear power station's employees are also distributed as a Poisson random variable, investigate the claim that the annual mean per employee is greater than 3. [A]

5 A random sample of 18 female computer operators each had their diastolic blood pressure measured to the nearest millimetre, with the following results:

$$57 \quad 64 \quad 77 \quad 82 \quad 66 \quad 94 \quad 72 \quad 83 \quad 61$$
$$72 \quad 65 \quad 89 \quad 54 \quad 73 \quad 55 \quad 67 \quad 71 \quad 68$$

(a) Stating any necessary distributional assumptions, show that there is no significant evidence to reject the hypothesis that the standard deviation of female computer operators' diastolic blood pressures is equal to that of the female population, namely 10 mm.

(b) Making appropriate use of the statement in (a), investigate the claim that the mean diastolic blood pressure of female computer operators differs from 75 mm.

6 The number of misprints per page in each national daily newspaper is known to follow a Poisson distribution. The mean number per page for the tabloid newspapers is 4. The Daily Planet, a quality newspaper, claims that, although its pages are much bigger and contain more text than those of the tabloid papers, its mean number of misprints per page is certainly fewer.

A random sample of 16 pages from recent editions of the Daily Planet results in the following numbers of misprints:

$$0 \quad 3 \quad 2 \quad 3 \quad 1 \quad 4 \quad 5 \quad 2 \quad 3 \quad 4 \quad 5 \quad 2 \quad 4 \quad 3 \quad 3 \quad 1$$

Investigate, at the 5% significance level, the Daily Planet's claim. [A]

7 Explain what is meant by the following terms when used in the context of a hypothesis test.

(a) Null and alternative hypotheses.

(b) Type 1 and Type 2 errors.

(c) One-tailed and two-tailed tests.

A new dietary treatment for a severe allergy is claimed to have a better cure rate than the accepted value of 60% for the well-established standard drug treatment. A random sample of 20 patients, suffering from the allergy, is given the new dietary treatment and as a result 17 are cured. Is the claim valid? [A]

8 The external diameter, in centimetres, of each of a random sample of 10 pistons manufactured on a particular machine was measured with the results below.

$$9.91 \quad 9.89 \quad 10.06 \quad 9.98 \quad 10.09$$
$$9.81 \quad 10.01 \quad 9.99 \quad 9.87 \quad 10.09$$

Stating any necessary assumptions, test the two distinct claims that piston rings manufactured on this machine have a mean external diameter of 10 cm with a variance of 0.005 cm^2. [A]

9 A sweet shop sells chocolates which appear, at first sight, to be identical. Of a random sample of 80 chocolates, 61 had hard centres and the rest soft centres. Test the hypothesis that 70% of chocolates have hard centres.

The chocolates are all in the shape of circular disks and the diameters, in millimetres, of the 19 soft-centred chocolates were as follows:

    279   263   284   277   281   269   266   271   262   275
    266   272   281   274   279   277   267   269   275

Assuming that the diameters of the soft-centred chocolates are normally distributed, test, at the 10% significance level, the hypothesis that their mean diameter is 275 mm.

What changes would you make to your test if it was known that the standard deviation of the diameters of soft-centred chocolates was 5 mm? [A]

10 It is known that repeated weighings of the same object on a particular chemical balance give readings which are normally distributed. Past evidence, using experienced operators, suggests that the mean is equal to the mass of the object and that the standard deviation is 0.25 mg.

A trainee operator makes seven repeated weighings of the same object, which is known to have a mass of 19.5 mg, and obtains the following readings:

    19.1   19.4   19.0   18.8   19.7   19.8   19.3

Is there any evidence that these results are more variable than those obtained by experienced operators?

Hence investigate whether or not the trainee operator's readings are biased. [A]

11 As part of a statistics project, students observed five private cars passing a college and counted the number which were carrying the driver only, with no passengers. This was repeated 80 times. The results for a particular student were as follows:

Number of cars with driver only	0	1	2	3	4	5
Number of times observed	0	3	12	27	26	12

Assuming a binomial model is appropriate, state the value of the parameter n and estimate the value of the parameter p.

Hence investigate the claim that more than 60% of cars contain the driver only. [A]

12 A car insurance company found that the average amount it was paying on bodywork claims in 1992 was £435 with a standard deviation of £141. The first six bodywork payments, in pounds, in 1993 were

548   209   534   198   789   633.

Stating clearly all necessary assumptions, has there been a significant change in the average and in the variability of payments in 1993 as compared to 1992? [A]

13 Before its annual overhaul, the mean operating time of an automatic machine was 100 s. After the overhaul, the following random sample of operating times, in seconds, was obtained:

90   97   101   92   101   95   95   98   96   95

Assuming that the time taken by the machine to perform the operation is a normally distributed random variable, investigate the claim that the overhaul has improved the machine's operation.

14 A nurseryman decided to keep records of the first year's growth of his pine seedlings. On the first occasion he found a mean growth of 11.5 cm with a standard deviation of 2.5 cm. The following year he used an experimental soil preparation for all his seedlings and the first year's growth of a random sample of eight of the seedlings was

7   23   19   25   11   18   17 and 15 cm.

(a) Assuming these data may be regarded as a random sample from a normal distribution, investigate at the 5% significance level, whether there has been a change in:
  (i) the standard deviation,
  (ii) the mean.

(b) Explain to the nurseryman why the conclusions in **(a)** cannot necessarily be attributed to the new soil preparation. [A]

15 The development engineer of a company making razors records the time it takes him to shave, on seven mornings, using a standard razor made by the company. The times, in seconds, were

217   210   254   237   232   228   243.

Assuming that this may be regarded as a random sample from a normal distribution, with mean μ and variance σ^2, test, at the 5% level of significance, the hypothesis that:

(a) $\sigma = 10$ s,

(b) $\mu = 240$ s. [A]

16 Packets of ground filter coffee have a nominal weight of 200 g. The distribution of weights may be assumed to be normal. A random sample of 30 packets had the following weights:

218	207	214	189	211	206	203	217	183	186
219	213	207	214	203	204	195	197	213	212
188	221	217	184	186	216	198	211	216	200

Investigate the assumption that the mean weight of all packets is 200 g.

Test the hypothesis that 15% of packets weigh less than 190 g. [A]

17 (a) The number of accidents per day on a stretch of motorway is known to have a Poisson distribution. Police claim that there is an average of more than one accident per day. Over a particular seven-day period there is a total of 13 accidents. Investigate the claim of the police.

(b) The results of a survey to establish the attitude of individuals to a particular proposal showed that three quarters of those interviewed were house owners. Of the 200 interviewed, only 12 of the 70 in favour of the proposal were not house owners. Test the hypothesis that the percentage of house owners in favour of the proposal is 40. [A]

18 The resistances (in ohms) of a sample from a batch of resistors were as follows:

2314	2456	2389	2361	2360	2332	2402

Stating any necessary assumptions, test the hypothesis that the true standard deviation of the resistors is 30 ohms.

Hence test the hypothesis that the actual mean resistance of the resistors is 2400 ohms. [A]

19 Explain **each** of the terms *null hypothesis*, *critical region* and *test statistic* as used in hypothesis testing.

Employees of a firm carrying out motorway maintenance are issued with brightly coloured waterproof jackets. These come in different sizes numbered 1 to 5. The last 40 jackets issued were of the following sizes.

2	3	3	1	3	4	2	4	3	2
5	4	1	2	1	3	2	4	5	5
2	4	4	1	5	3	3	2	2	3
1	3	4	3	3	2	5	1	4	4

Assuming that the 40 employees may be regarded as a random sample of all employees, test the hypothesis, at the 5% significance level, that 40% of all employees require size 3.

Key point summary

1 (a) To test hypotheses about a normal population variance, σ^2, or standard deviation, σ, use $\qquad$ *p 36*

$$\frac{(n-1)S^2}{\sigma^2} \sim \chi^2_{n-1}.$$

(b) To test hypotheses about a normal population mean, μ, use $\qquad$ *p 35*

$$\frac{\overline{X} - \mu}{\dfrac{S}{\sqrt{n}}} \sim t_{n-1}.$$

2 To test hypotheses about a binomial population proportion, p, either:

(a) determine the cumulative binomial probability of $B(n, p)$, or

(b) determine the cumulative Poisson probability of $Po(\lambda = np)$ when $n \geqslant 50$, $p < 0.1$ (or $p > 0.9$), or

(c) use

$$\frac{\hat{P} - p}{\sqrt{\dfrac{p(1-p)}{n}}} \sim N(0, 1)$$

when $n \geqslant 50$ and $np \geqslant 10$. $\qquad$ *p 42*

3 To test hypotheses about a Poisson population mean λ, either

(a) determine the cumulative Poisson probability of $Po(\lambda)$, or

(b) use

$$\frac{\hat{\lambda} - \lambda}{\sqrt{\lambda}} \sim N(0, 1)$$

when $\lambda > 10$. $\qquad$ *p 44*

Test yourself	What to review

1 A flooring company suspects that some of the complaints it has received recently, regarding a major ceramic flooring contract, are due to a high level of variation in the thickness of the tiles.

Sections 4.1 and 4.2

To investigate this suspicion the thickness, in millimetres, is measured for each tile in a random sample of 15 tiles taken from the same batch as those used in the contract. From these an unbiased estimate of the population variance is calculated correctly to be $0.001\,98\,\text{mm}^2$.

The tile manufacturer claims that the population standard deviation of tile thickness is $0.03\,\text{mm}$.

(a) Assuming the tile thickness to be approximately normally distributed, determine whether the flooring company's suspicion of a high level of variation in the thickness of the tiles is justified. Use the 5% significance level.

(b) State the type of error that may have been made in your conclusion to the hypothesis test in **(a)**, and write down its associated probability.

2 In the production of cough syrup it is important to control both the average level and the variability of each ingredient.

Sections 4.1 and 4.2

The data below show the amount, $x\,\text{mg}$, of codeine in each of a random sample of twelve $200\,\text{ml}$ bottles of a particular cough syrup.

59.3	59.8	61.2	59.3	60.8	60.8
61.1	60.8	60.4	58.8	60.6	58.9

Codeine content may be assumed to be normally distributed.

(a) Test, at the 5% level of significance, the hypothesis that the standard deviation of codeine content in $200\,\text{ml}$ bottles of the cough syrup is $1\,\text{mg}$.

(b) Hence investigate, again at the 5% level of significance, the claim that the mean codeine content in $200\,\text{ml}$ bottles of this cough syrup is more than $60\,\text{mg}$.

Test yourself (*continued*)	What to review

3 A midwife claims that when attempting to predict the sex of an unborn baby from the shape of the mother during pregnancy, she is correct more often than not. The claim is to be investigated using the 1% level of significance.

Section 4.3

   (a) Use the table of cumulative binomial probabilities to show that a sample of six predictions would be insufficient for this purpose.

   (b) In one week the midwife predicted the sex of 13 babies, and in 11 of these predictions proved to be correct. Use this result to investigate her claim.

   (c) As part of an extensive study over several months, the midwife predicted the sex of 200 babies, and 114 of these predictions proved to be correct. Use this result to reinvestigate her claim.

4 Observation of a random sample of 250 cars leaving a motorway at an urban intersection during the morning rush hour revealed that 168 contained only the driver.

Section 4.3

Stating null and alternative hypotheses, investigate, at the 5% level of significance, the claim that more than 60 per cent of cars leaving the motorway at this urban intersection during the morning rush hour contain only the driver.

5 The number of email messages per hour received by a manager between 9.00 a.m. and 5.00 p.m. on Mondays to Fridays may be modelled by a Poisson distribution. On a randomly chosen Tuesday, the manager received 16 email messages. Test, at the 10% level of significance, the hypothesis that the mean number of email messages per hour received by the manager is 1.25.

Section 4.4

6 The number of telephone calls Mr Fish receives at home per day has a mean of 2.4. Assume this situation may be modelled by a Poisson distribution.

Section 4.4

After an aggressive advertising campaign, during which the cost of telephone calls was reduced, Mrs Fish claimed that the number of telephone calls had increased.

   (a) On a day chosen at random, Mr Fish received five telephone calls. Investigate, at the 5% level of significance, Mrs Fish's claim.

   (b) In a random sample of 30 days over the next few months, Mr Fish received 90 telephone calls. Use a normal approximation to reinvestigate Mrs Fish's claim, again at the 5% level of significance.

1 (a) $\chi^2 = 30.8$, c.v. 23.685, suspicion justified;
  (b) Type 1, 5%.

2 (a) $\chi^2 = 8.49$, c.v. 3.816 and 21.920, accept $\sigma = 1\,\text{mg}$;
  (b) $z = 0.52$, c.v. ±1.96, accept $\mu = 60\,\text{mg}$,
     (or $t = 0.59$, c.v. ±2.201, accept $\mu = 60\,\text{mg}$).

3 (a) $P(X = 6 \mid p = 0.5) = 0.0156$, impossible to reject at 1% level
     even if all six predictions correct;
  (b) $P(Y \geqslant 11 \mid p = 0.5) = 0.0112$, claim not substantiated at 1%
     level (but substantiated at very slightly higher significance
     level);
  (c) $z = 1.98$, c.v. 2.3263, claim not substantiated.

4 $z = 2.32$, c.v. 1.6449, $p > 60\%$.

5 $P(X \geqslant 16 \mid \lambda = 10) = 0.0487$, mean $\neq 1.25$ (>1.25).

6 (a) $P(X \geqslant 5 \mid \lambda = 2.4) = 0.0959$, accept no increase;
  (b) $z = 2.12$, c.v. 1.6449, mean increased.

CHAPTER 5

Hypothesis testing: two-sample tests

Learning objectives

After studying this chapter you should be able to:

- carry out a test for the equality of two normal population variances
- carry out tests for the equality of (or for a given difference in) two normal population means using information from two independent samples.

5

5.1 Introduction

In the previous chapter, tests were described for a parameter of a single population. In this chapter, some of these tests will be developed, and new ones introduced, to test for the equality of a parameter in two populations.

It is a well-known and frequently stated fact that, on average, men are significantly taller than women. Less well-known is the fact that the variability in men's heights is greater than that in women's heights.

In this chapter you will see how to investigate whether two normal populations differ on average and whether they differ in variability.

5.2 Two normal population variances

One possible question arising from data collected on height might be: 'Is the variability in height the same for men and women?' This question may be formulated as the following two hypotheses.

H_0: $\sigma_x^2 = \sigma_y^2$ (x = male, y = female)
H_1: $\sigma_x^2 \neq \sigma_y^2$ (where σ^2 denotes population variance)

It is important to note that, although an assumption of normal populations is required for such tests, no assumption is required as to the equality or otherwise of the population means μ_x and μ_y.

In section 4.2, a statistic based upon the variance estimate, S^2, was used in testing hypotheses concerning a single normal population variance (or standard deviation). Here, when testing the equality of two independent normal population variances (or standard deviations), the statistic used is the ratio of the two variances estimates.

In fact, if
S_x^2 denotes the variance estimate from a sample of size n_x from a normal population with variance σ_x^2
and
S_y^2 denotes the variance estimate from a sample of size n_y from a normal population with variance σ_y^2,
then

$$\frac{S_x^2/\sigma_x^2}{S_y^2/\sigma_y^2} \sim F_{n_x-1,\,n_y-1}$$

(*F*-distribution with $v_1 = n_x - 1$ and $v_2 = n_y - 1$ degrees of freedom.)

> This formula is given in the AQA booklet of formulae and tables.

The *F*-distribution was developed by the American statistician, G. W. Snedecor, and so named in honour of R. A. Fisher (1890–1962), an eminent British statistician, who originally discovered the distribution in a slightly different form.

The distribution depends on the two parameters v_1 and v_2 for its shape and, except for large values of both, is positively skewed (like the χ^2-distribution). The distribution function for F exists for the range zero to infinity and is very complicated. The mean of F_{v_1,v_2} exists only for $v_2 > 2$ and is given by $\dfrac{v_2}{(v_2 - 2)}$. The variance exists only for $v_2 > 4$ and is a complicated function of v_1 and v_2.

Assuming $H_0: \sigma_x^2 = \sigma_y^2$, is true, then

$$F = \frac{S_x^2}{S_y^2} \sim F_{n_x-1,\,n_y-1}$$

and, **adopting the convention of always putting the larger S^2 in the numerator**, will result in H_0 being rejected when F becomes significantly large.

This significance can be assessed by making reference to tables of **upper percentage points** of the *F*-distribution.
For example:

the upper 5.0% point of $F_{9,14}$ is 2.646,

the upper 0.5% point of $F_{4,6}$ is 12.028.

Note that, for larger values of v_1 and/or v_2, linear interpolation may be necessary to obtain accurate percentage points.

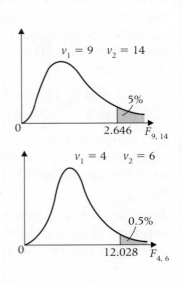

Worked example 5.1

A random sample of 10 hot drinks from Dispenser A had a mean volume of 203 ml and a standard deviation, s, of 3 ml. A random sample of 15 hot drinks from Dispenser B gave corresponding values of 206 ml and 5 ml. The amount dispensed by each machine may be assumed to be normally distributed. Test, at the 5% significance level, the hypothesis that there is no difference in the variability of the volume dispensed by the two machines.

Solution

H_0: $\sigma_A^2 = \sigma_B^2$
H_1: $\sigma_A^2 \neq \sigma_B^2$ (two-tailed)
Significance level, $\alpha = 0.05$.

Since $s_B > s_A$ and the larger value is always placed in the numerator, $v_1 = n_B - 1 = 14$ and $v_2 = n_A - 1 = 9$.

Using interpolation, **the upper 2.5% point** for

$$F_{14,9} = F_{12,9} - \tfrac{2}{3}(F_{12,9} - F_{15,9})$$
$$= 3.868 - \tfrac{2}{3}(3.868 - 3.769)$$
$$= 3.802$$

Thus the critical region is $F > 3.802$

The test statistic is

$$F = \frac{s_B^2}{s_A^2} = \frac{5^2}{3^2} = 2.78$$

This value does not lie in the critical region. Thus there is no evidence, at the 5% level of significance, of a difference in the variability of the volume dispensed by the two machines.

> Note that for a 5% two-tailed test there is a 2.5% critical region in the lower tail as well as the region shown. As we always put the larger s^2 in the numerator, this lower critical region can be ignored.

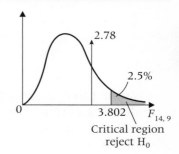

> Note that since 2.78 is less than both 3.868 and 3.769, H_0 could be accepted in this case, without carrying out the interpolation.

EXERCISE 5A

1 An investigation was conducted into the dust content in the flue gases of two types of solid-fuel boilers. Thirteen boilers of type A and nine boilers of type B were used under identical fuelling and extraction conditions. Over a similar period, the following quantities, in grams, of dust were deposited in similar traps inserted in each of the 22 flues.

Type A	73.1	56.4	82.1	67.2
	78.7	75.1	48.0	
	53.3	55.5	61.5	
	60.6	55.2	63.1	
Type B	53.0	39.3	55.8	
	58.8	41.2	66.6	
	46.0	56.4	58.9	

Assuming that these independent samples come from normal populations, test for an equality of population variances. [A]

2 Korn Krispies are a type of breakfast cereal. They are packed in boxes with a nominal net mass of 296 g. Owing to overwhelming demand, the manufacturers have installed a new and faster machine to fill the boxes with cereal. However, to meet government regulations, amongst other things, the variability in the packed masses of these boxes should not increase above present levels. The table below gives the masses of a random sample of ten boxes of cereal from the original packing machine, and the masses of a random sample of twelve boxes of cereal from the new machine.

Original machine		New machine	
301.0	292.4	295.3	320.4
293.6	298.7	289.4	312.2
291.1	285.1	288.5	292.9
305.1	290.0	299.8	300.2
297.0	302.2	293.6	276.3
		308.9	280.3

Assuming that these independent samples came from underlying normal populations, use the 5% level of significance to determine whether an increase in variance has occurred. [A]

3 In a research study aimed at improving the design of bus cabs it was necessary to measure the functional arm reach of bus drivers. In a pilot study, a research worker made this measurement on a random sample of ten bus drivers from a large depot, and next day her assistant made this measurement on a random sample of eight bus drivers from the same depot. The results, in millimetres, were as follows:

Research worker	730	698	712	686	724
	711	679	762	683	673
Assistant	701	642	651	700	672
	674	656	649		

Assuming a normal distribution for functional arm reach, test, at the 10% significance level, whether the samples could have come from populations with the same variance. [A]

4 As part of a research study into pattern recognition, subjects were asked to examine a picture and see if they could distinguish a word. The picture contained the word 'technology' written backwards and camouflaged by an elaborate pattern. Of the 23 librarians who took part, 11 succeeded in recognising the word whilst of 19 designers, 13 succeeded. The times, in seconds, for the successful subjects to recognise the word were as follows:

Librarians	55	18	99	54	87	11
	62	68	27	90	57	
Designers	23	69	34	27	51	29	45
	42	48	74	31	30	31	

Stating any necessary assumptions, investigate the hypothesis that the variability of times for librarians significantly exceeds that for designers. [A]

5 The light attenuation of trees may be measured by photometric methods, which are very time consuming, or by photographic techniques which are much quicker. The light attenuation of an oak tree was repeatedly measured by both methods independently. The following results, expressed as percentages, were obtained.

Photometric	85.6	86.1	86.5	85.1	86.8	87.3	
Photographic	82.4	84.7	86.1	87.2	82.4	85.8	84.4

Assuming normal distributions, investigate at the 5% level of significance whether there is a difference in the variability of the two methods. [A]

6 A firm is to buy a fleet of cars for use by its salesmen and wishes to choose between two alternative models, A and B. It places an advertisement in a local paper offering 20 l of petrol free to anyone who has bought a new car of either model in the last year. The offer is conditional on being willing to answer a questionnaire and to note how far the car goes, under typical driving conditions, on the free petrol supplied. The following data were obtained.

	Km driven on 20 l of petrol			
Model A	187	218	173	235
Model B	157	198	154	184
	202	174	146	173

Assuming these data to be random samples from two normal populations, test whether the population variances may be assumed equal. [A]

5.3 Two normal population means – case 1

Independent samples and known population variances – normal test

It is claimed that Brand A size D alkaline batteries last longer than those of Brand B.

All mass-produced articles are liable to random variation which should be monitored and controlled, but cannot be eliminated entirely. Such variation is generally assumed, with good cause, to be approximately normally distributed. Thus it is quite possible that, whilst the claim may be true **on average**, it is not the case for every Brand A size D alkaline battery.

Investigating claims of a population mean difference generally requires a comparison of two sample means; in the example above, measuring the lifetimes of all Brand A (and B) battery lifetimes would leave none for sale!

As noted earlier, the variance of a sample mean depends upon the sample size and the variance of the population from which the sample is selected. Consequently the sizes of the two samples and the variances of the two populations will influence the comparison of sample means.

From earlier work you have seen that:

(a) if $X \sim N(\mu, \sigma^2)$, then $\overline{X} \sim N\left(\mu, \dfrac{\sigma^2}{n}\right)$;

(b) if $X \sim N(\mu_x, \sigma_x^2)$ independent of $Y \sim N(\mu_y, \sigma_y^2)$,

then $X - Y \sim N(\mu_x - \mu_y, \sigma_x^2 + \sigma_y^2)$.

Combining these two results gives

$$\overline{X} - \overline{Y} \sim N\left(\mu_x - \mu_y, \frac{\sigma_x^2}{n_x} + \frac{\sigma_y^2}{n_y}\right)$$

and hence

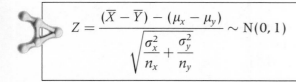

$$Z = \frac{(\overline{X} - \overline{Y}) - (\mu_x - \mu_y)}{\sqrt{\dfrac{\sigma_x^2}{n_x} + \dfrac{\sigma_y^2}{n_y}}} \sim N(0, 1)$$

This formula is given in the AQA booklet of formulae and tables.

This result can be used to test the equality of (or given difference in) two normal population means, μ_x and μ_y, based upon independent random samples.

It is perhaps worth noting here that for $n_x > 30$ and $n_y > 30$, the requirement of normal populations can be relaxed as a result of the Central Limit Theorem. Also, in such cases, s_x^2 and s_y^2, may be used as estimates of σ_x^2 and σ_y^2, respectively, so providing an approximate z-statistic.

Worked example 5.2

The alkalinity, in milligrams per litre, of water in the upper reaches of rivers in a particular region is known to be normally distributed with a standard deviation of 10. Alkalinity readings in the lower reaches of rivers in the same region are also known to be normally distributed, but with a standard deviation of 25.

Ten alkalinity readings are made in the upper reaches of a river in the region and 15 in the lower reaches of the same river with the following results:

Upper reaches	91	75	91	88	94	63	86	77	71	69
Lower reaches	86	95	135	121	68	64	113	108	79	62
	143	108	121	85	97					

Investigate, at the 1% level of significance, the claim that the true mean alkalinity of water in the lower reaches of this river is greater than that in the upper reaches.

Solution

H_0: $\mu_1 = \mu_2$ (1 = lower, 2 = upper)

H_1: $\mu_1 > \mu_2$ (one-tailed)

Significance level, $\alpha = 0.01$

Critical region, $z > 2.3263$

Under H_0, the test statistic is

$$z = \frac{(\bar{x}_1 - \bar{x}_2)}{\sqrt{\dfrac{\sigma_1{}^2}{n_1} + \dfrac{\sigma_2{}^2}{n_2}}}$$

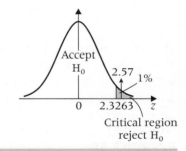

$\mu_1 - \mu_2 = 0$

Calculation gives $\bar{x}_1 = \dfrac{1485}{15} = 99.0$ and $\bar{x}_2 = \dfrac{805}{10} = 80.5$,

so

$$z = \frac{(99.0 - 80.5)}{\sqrt{\dfrac{25^2}{15} + \dfrac{10^2}{10}}} = 2.57$$

This value does lie in the critical region so H_0 is rejected. Thus there is evidence, at the 1% level of significance, to suggest that the true mean alkalinity of water in the lower reaches of the river is greater than that in the upper reaches.

Worked example 5.3

Sometimes, rather than requiring a test for the equality of two means, a test is required for a specified difference between them. Thus, for example, suppose the request in Worked example 5.2 was: 'Investigate, at the 1% level of significance, the claim that the true mean alkalinity of water in the lower reaches of this river is more than $10\,\text{mg}\,\text{l}^{-1}$ more than that in the upper reaches.'

Solution

H_0: $\mu_1 = \mu_2 + 10$ ($1 = $ lower, $2 = $ upper)

H_1: $\mu_1 > \mu_2 + 10$ (one-tailed)

Significance level, $\alpha = 0.01$

Critical region, $z > 2.3263$

Under H_0, the test statistic is

$$z = \frac{(\bar{x}_1 - \bar{x}_2) - 10}{\sqrt{\dfrac{\sigma_1^{\,2}}{n_1} + \dfrac{\sigma_2^{\,2}}{n_2}}}$$

> Note that if H_0 is true, then $\mu_1 - \mu_2 = 10$.

giving

$$z = \frac{(99.0 - 80.5) - 10}{\sqrt{\dfrac{25^2}{15} + \dfrac{10^2}{10}}} = 1.18$$

This value does not lie in the critical region so H_0 is not rejected. Thus there is no evidence, at the 1% level of significance, to suggest that the true mean alkalinity of water in the lower reaches of the river is more than $10\,\text{mg}\,\text{l}^{-1}$ more than that in the upper reaches.

EXERCISE 5B

1 The weight of crisps delivered into bags by a machine is known to be normally distributed with a standard deviation of 0.5 g.

Prior to a minor overhaul of the machine, the contents, in grams, of a random sample of six bags are as follows:

151.7   152.6   150.8   151.9   152.3   151.5

After the overhaul, which from past experience is known not to affect the standard deviation, the contents of a random sample of twelve bags were measured with the results below.

151.1   150.7   149.0   150.3   151.3   151.4
150.8   149.5   150.2   150.6   150.9   151.3

Test, at the 5% significance level, the hypothesis that the minor overhaul has had no effect on the mean mass of crisps delivered by the machine.

2 A firm obtains its supply of steel wire of a particular gauge from each of two manufacturers, *A* and *B*. The firm suspects that the mean breaking strength, in newtons (N), of wire from manufacturer *A* differs from that supplied by manufacturer *B*.

The table below shows the breaking strengths of random samples of wire from each of the two manufacturers.

A	80.5	83.1	73.6	70.4	68.9	71.6	82.3	78.6	73.4
B	71.4	86.2	81.4	72.3	78.9	80.3	81.4	78.0	

Assuming all such breaking strengths to be normally distributed with a standard deviation of 5 N, investigate the firm's suspicion.

3 The manager of a lemonade bottling plant is interested in comparing the performance of two production lines, one of which has only recently been installed. For each line she selects 10 one-hour periods at random and records the number of crates completed in each hour. The table below gives the results.

Production line	Number of crates completed per hour									
1 (new)	78	87	79	82	87	81	85	80	82	83
2 (old)	74	77	78	70	87	83	76	78	81	76

From past experience with this kind of equipment it is known that the variance in these figures will be 10 for Line 1 and 25 for Line 2. Assuming that these samples came from normal populations with these variances, test the hypothesis that the two populations have the same mean. [A]

4 Rice Pops are a type of breakfast cereal which is packed into boxes, with a quoted net mass of 296 g, by one of two different filling machines. The mass of cereal delivered by filling machine A, an old machine, is known to be normally distributed with a standard deviation of 5 g. The mass of cereal delivered by machine B, a new machine, is also known to be normally distributed but with a standard deviation of 3 g. The table below shows the net masses, in grams, of a random sample of 12 boxes filled by machine A and of a random sample of 15 boxes filled by machine B.

Boxes filled by machine A			Boxes filled by machine B		
296	296	302	296	297	299
304	300	306	301	297	299
305	297	307	298	302	304
303	299	306	298	299	303
			297	296	299

Test the hypothesis that there is no significant difference in the mean mass of cereal delivered by the two filling machines. [A]

5 During the first three months of 1993 a technician was timed for the repair of an electronic instrument on 12 separate occasions. In the same period a trainee technician was timed for the repair of a similar instrument on 14 occasions. These times, in minutes, are given in the table below.

Technician	344	278	267	234	212	271	
	341	391	176	164	214	399	
Trainee	279	351	282	280	258	267	312
	357	322	249	228	315	311	341

(a) Assuming that these observations may be regarded as independent random samples from normal populations with known standard deviations of 80 minutes (for the technician) and 40 minutes (for the trainee technician), test the hypothesis that there is no difference in the mean times.

(b) Subsequently it was learned that the times for the trainee were incorrectly recorded and that each of the values above is 30 minutes too quick. What, if any, difference does this make to the result of the test you have just completed? [A]

6 James and his sister, Alison, each deliver 30 papers on their evening paper rounds and each are paid the same amount. One evening Alison claims this system of equal payment to be unfair as her round takes, on average, five minutes longer than that of her brother. To test her claim their father, unknown to them, records their delivery times for 12 consecutive days. One of Alison's times had to be discounted as the front tyre of her bicycle was punctured. The recorded times, in minutes, were as shown below.

	Delivery times (minutes)										
James	45	30	39	32	34	43	38	35	43	39	32	34
Alison	53	46	43	49	42	53	47	40	37	45	40	

Assuming each child's delivery times are normally distributed with the same known standard deviation of five minutes, investigate whether Alison's claim is justified, using a 5% level of significance. [A]

5.4 Two normal population means – case 2

Independent samples and unknown but equal population variances – t-test

In section 5.3 the test statistic z required that the two populations are normal with known variances, σ_x^2 and σ_y^2. If, however, both sample sizes are greater than 30, it was stated that s_x^2 and s_y^2 may be used as estimates to provide an approximate z-statistic.

In most practical situations, the population variances are unknown and the sample sizes are less than 30.

If it may be assumed, or has been confirmed using the *F*-test of section 5.2, that the population variances are equal, but unknown, then a test is available for all sample sizes if the two populations are normal. (For small samples from normal populations with unknown and unequal variances, an involved approximate *t*-test is available, but it is outside the scope of this text.)

Returning to the test statistic of section 5.3, defined by

$$Z = \frac{(\overline{X} - \overline{Y}) - (\mu_x - \mu_y)}{\sqrt{\dfrac{\sigma_x^2}{n_x} + \dfrac{\sigma_y^2}{n_y}}}$$

then, if $\sigma_x^2 = \sigma_y^2 = \sigma^2$ (unknown), it follows that

$$Z = \frac{(\overline{X} - \overline{Y}) - (\mu_x - \mu_y)}{\sqrt{\sigma^2 \left(\dfrac{1}{n_x} + \dfrac{1}{n_y}\right)}}$$

s_x^2 and s_y^2 are estimates of σ^2, so this information can be combined to form a pooled (weighted) estimate of variance defined by:

$$s_p^2 = \frac{(n_x - 1)s_x^2 + (n_y - 1)s_y^2}{n_x + n_y - 2}$$

This formula is given in the AQA booklet of formulae and tables.

From section 4.2 of S4, it was seen that when σ^2 is replaced by s^2 in a *z*-statistic, the result is a *t*-statistic.

Hence

$$\frac{(\overline{X} - \overline{Y}) - (\mu_x - \mu_y)}{\sqrt{s_p^2 \left(\dfrac{1}{n_x} + \dfrac{1}{n_y}\right)}} \sim t_{n_x + n_y - 2}$$

This formula is given in the AQA booklet of formulae and tables.

(a *t*-distribution with $v = n_x + n_y - 2$ degrees of freedom)

Worked example 5.4

Mr Brown is the owner of a small bakery in a large town. He believes that the smell of fresh baking will encourage customers to purchase goods from his bakery. To investigate this belief, he records the daily sales for 10 days when all the bakery's windows are open, and the daily sales for another 10 days when all the windows are closed. The following sales, in pounds sterling, are recorded.

Windows open	202.0	204.5	207.0	215.5	190.8
	215.6	208.8	187.8	204.1	185.7
Windows closed	193.5	192.2	199.4	177.6	205.4
	200.6	181.8	169.2	172.2	192.8

Assuming that these data may be deemed to be random samples from normal populations with the same variance, investigate the baker's belief.

Solution

$H_0: \mu_x = \mu_y \qquad (x = \text{open}, y = \text{closed})$

$H_1: \mu_x > \mu_y \qquad \text{(one-tailed)}$

Significance level, $\alpha = 0.05$ (say)

Degrees of freedom, $v = 10 + 10 - 2 = 18$

Critical region, $t > 1.734$

Under H_0, the test statistic is

$$t = \frac{\bar{x} - \bar{y}}{\sqrt{s_p^2 \left(\frac{1}{n_x} + \frac{1}{n_y} \right)}}$$

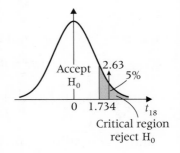

Calculation gives

$$\bar{x} = 202.18, \ s_x^2 = 115.7284$$

and $\quad \bar{y} = 188.47, \ s_y^2 = 156.6534$

Hence $\quad s_p^2 = \dfrac{9 \times 115.7284 + 9 \times 156.6534}{10 + 10 - 2}$

$$= \frac{115.7284 + 156.6534}{2}$$

so $\quad s_p^2 = 136.1909$

Note that when $n_x = n_y$, s_p^2 is the average of s_x^2 and s_y^2.

Thus $\quad t = \dfrac{202.18 - 188.47}{\sqrt{136.1909 \left(\dfrac{1}{10} + \dfrac{1}{10} \right)}} = 2.63$

This value does lie in the critical region so H_0 is rejected. Thus there is evidence, at the 5% level of significance, to suggest that the smell of fresh baking will encourage customers to purchase goods from Mr Brown's bakery.

Worked example 5.5

Referring back to Worked example 5.1 concerning the two drink dispensers, test, at the 5% level of significance, the hypothesis that there is no difference in the mean volume dispensed by the two machines.

Solution

$H_0: \mu_A = \mu_B$

$H_1: \mu_A \neq \mu_B$ (two-tailed)

Significance level, $\alpha = 0.05$

Degrees of freedom, $v = 10 + 15 - 2 = 23$

Critical region, $t < -1.714$ or $t > 1.714$

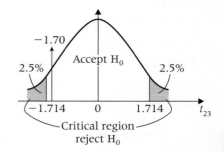

Under H_0, the test statistic is

$$t = \frac{\bar{x}_A - \bar{x}_B}{\sqrt{s_p^2 \left(\dfrac{1}{n_A} + \dfrac{1}{n_B} \right)}}$$

$\bar{x}_A = 203$, $s_A = 3$ and $\bar{x}_B = 206$, $s_B = 5$

Hence

$$s_p^2 = \frac{9 \times 3^2 + 14 \times 5^2}{10 + 15 - 2} = 18.7391$$

Thus $t = \dfrac{203 - 206}{\sqrt{18.7391 \left(\dfrac{1}{10} + \dfrac{1}{15} \right)}} = -1.70$

This value does not lie in the critical region so H_0 is not rejected. Thus there is no evidence, at the 5% level of significance, to suggest that there is a difference in the mean volume dispensed by the two machines.

EXERCISE 5C

1 A microbiologist wishes to determine whether there is any difference in the time it takes to make yogurt from two different starters; *lactobacillus acidophilus* (A) and *bulgarius* (B). Seven batches of yogurt were made with each of the starters. The table below shows the time taken, in hours, to make each batch.

Starter A	6.8	6.3	7.4	6.1	8.2	7.3	6.9
Starter B	6.1	6.4	5.7	5.5	6.9	6.3	6.7

Assuming that both sets of times may be considered to be random samples from normal populations with the same variance, test the hypothesis that the mean time taken to make yogurt is the same for both starters.

2 Referring to question 1 of exercise 5A, test for an equality of population means. [A]

3 Referring to question 3 of exercise 5A, show that, at the 1% significance level, the hypothesis that the samples are from populations with equal means is rejected. [A]

4 Referring to question 5 of exercise 5A, determine, at the 5% significance level, whether there is a difference in the mean measurement by the two methods. [A]

5 Referring to question 6 of exercise 5A, test whether the population means may be assumed equal. [A]

6 A new chemical process is developed for the manufacture of nickel–cadmium batteries. The company believes that this new process will increase the mean lifetime of a battery by five hours as compared to that of batteries produced by the old process. Sixteen batteries produced by the old process were randomly selected and the mean and the standard deviation of the lifetimes of these batteries were 105.2 hours and 9.1 hours, respectively. Fifteen batteries produced by the new process were also randomly selected and calculations gave corresponding values of 112.4 and 8.3 hours.

Assuming all battery lifetimes to be normally distributed, test at the 5% significance level whether there is:

(a) a difference in the variability of the two processes,

(b) an increase of five hours in the mean lifetime of batteries produced by the new process as compared to that of batteries produced by the old process.

MIXED EXERCISE

1 Transporting frozen food by lorry requires that the temperature is maintained within a narrow range. If the temperature is too low, extra fuel is consumed and unnecessary costs are incurred. If the temperature is too high, health standards are violated and there is a danger of bacterial contamination and food wastage.

Two models, A and B, of refrigeration unit were being compared for their variation from a given temperature setting. A special sensor, attached to each unit, took readings at irregular intervals.

For model A, the estimated variance, s_A^2, based upon 16 readings was $3.78°C^2$. For model B, the estimated variance, s_B^2, based upon 12 readings was $1.40°C^2$. Each set of readings may be assumed to come from a normal distribution.

Test, at the 5% level of significance, the claim that there is no difference between the two models of refrigeration unit with respect to temperature variability. [A]

2 A computer salesperson travels regularly between her home in Teesside and the area office in Merseyside. She generally leaves home around 6.45 a.m. and leaves the area office for the return journey at about 5.00 p.m.

An analysis of a random sample of ten journeys from Teesside to Merseyside resulted in an estimated variance, s^2, of 120 minutes^2. For a random sample of eight journeys from Merseyside to Teesside, the estimated variance was 144 minutes^2.

Assuming that, for each direction of travel, journey times are normally distributed, investigate the claim that there is no difference in the variability of the journey times for the two directions of travel. [A]

3 The vitamin content of the flesh of each of a random sample of eight oranges and of a random sample of five lemons was measured. The results are given in milligrams per 10 grams.

Oranges	1.14	1.59	1.57	1.33	1.08	1.27	1.43	1.36
Lemons	1.04	0.95	0.63	1.62	1.11			

Assuming vitamin content to be normally distributed, test the hypothesis that both samples come from populations with the same variance. [A]

4 Over a certain period of time, a random sample of 15 private subscribers connected to telephone exchange X used a total of 7980 units. Over the same period of time, a random sample of 20 private subscribers connected to exchange Y used a total of 10 220 units. It is known that, for both exchanges, the numbers of units used by private subscribers during the period are normally distributed with standard deviation 100.

Test the hypothesis that there is no difference between the mean number of units used by private subscribers at exchanges X and Y.

5 An economist believes that a typical basket of weekly provisions, purchased by a family of four, costs more in Southville than it does in Nortown. Six stores were randomly selected in each of these two cities and the following costs, for identical baskets of provisions, were observed.

Southville	12.32	13.10	12.11	12.84	12.52	12.71
Nortown	11.95	11.84	12.22	12.67	11.53	12.03

Assuming costs in both towns to be normally distributed with the same variance, investigate the economist's belief. [A]

6 A high nitrate intake in food consumption is suspected of retarding the growth of some animals. The following data are the results of an experiment to measure the percentage gain in mass of young laboratory mice given either a standard diet (A) or an extra 200 parts per million of nitrate in their diet (B).

A	18.2	25.8	16.8	14.9	19.6	26.5	17.5
B	13.4	18.8	20.5	6.5	22.2	15.0	12.2
	14.3	18.0	15.1				

Assuming that both percentages are normally distributed with a standard deviation of 4.5, investigate, at the 1% level of significance, the claim that a high nitrate intake retards the mean percentage gain in mass of mice.

After the experiment was performed it was discovered that the laboratory mice used were not a homogeneous population. In fact, most of the mice in the control group were appreciably heavier than those in the experimental group. Discuss briefly the possible effect of this information on the validity of your analysis. [A]

7 An online catalogue of books is being introduced into a college library. Formerly the catalogue was held on microfiche. To test the new system, students were selected at random and asked to obtain some specified information from the microfiche catalogue and a further sample of students was asked to obtain the same information from the online catalogue. The times, in seconds, were as follows:

Microfiche	68	91	71	96	97	75		
Online	85	69	93	79	117	79	78	102

(a) Assuming normal distributions, determine, at the 5% significance level, whether there is a difference in:
   (i) the standard deviations of times for the two methods,
   (ii) the means of the times for the two methods.

(b) One student had taken 297 s to obtain the information using the online catalogue due to an initial misunderstanding of how to use the equipment. It had been decided to exclude this result from the data above. Comment on this decision and on the effect the inclusion of this result would have had on the assumptions you made in carrying out the test in **(a)(ii)**. [A]

8 It is claimed that Examiner V is more severe than Examiner W. This claim is based upon an analysis of the marks awarded by each examiner to independent random samples of scripts from a particular examination which had been marked by the two examiners. Some details of the marks awarded are as follows.

	Sample size	Sum of marks
Examiner V	25	1060
Examiner W	15	819

Investigate the claim that Examiner W awards, on average, more marks than Examiner V, assuming all marks are normally distributed with a standard deviation of 15.

9 A large consignment of similarly graded apples arrived at a company's warehouse for distribution to retail outlets. Two varieties were chosen and a random sample of each had their masses, in grams, measured. The results are tabulated below.

Variety I	110.5	89.6	89.1	85.6	115.0	98.2
	113.1	92.0	104.3	100.7	97.5	106.1
Variety II	125.6	118.3	118.0	110.8	116.5	108.7
	108.2	104.4	114.4	98.4	111.2	

Assuming that these independent samples came from underlying normal populations, use the 5% significance level to test the hypothesis that the population variances are the same.

Further, use the 5% level of significance to test the hypothesis that the population means are the same.

Later it transpired that the measuring device used to determine the masses was inaccurate. The true masses of the 23 apples considered were all 10 g more than the results given above. What effect do you think this information will have on the test results and why? (Further tests are not required.) [A]

10 Industrial waste dumped in rivers reduces the amount of dissolved oxygen in the water. A factory was suspected of illegally dumping waste in a river. Samples of water were taken from the river, six above the factory and eight below the factory, and the dissolved oxygen content in parts per million (ppm) was as follows.

Above factory	4.9	5.1	4.7	5.0	5.3	4.6		
Below factory	3.8	4.9	4.0	3.6	5.0	3.4	3.5	3.9

Making any necessary assumptions, investigate, at the 5% significance level, whether:

(a) the variability of the dissolved oxygen content is the same above and below the factory,

(b) the mean of the dissolved oxygen content is less below than above the factory. [A]

11 The manager of a road haulage firm records the time, in minutes, taken on six occasions for a lorry to travel from the depot to a particular customer's factory. Roadworks are due to start on the usual route so the manager decides to try an alternative route and records the times, in minutes, of eight journeys on this alternative route.

Old route	34	45	36	48	49	38		
Alternative route	43	35	47	39	58	40	39	51

Investigate, at the 5% significance level, whether there is a difference in:

(a) the variances of the times taken on the two routes,

(b) the means of the times taken on the two routes.

One driver had taken 99 minutes on the alternative route. Investigation showed that this was due to losing his way and it was decided to exclude this result from the above tests. Comment on this decision and state what assumptions may have been violated if the result had been included in the analysis. [A]

12 Celebrity endorsement of a product is a common advertising technique.

In one study, a randomly selected group of 125 people was shown a TV commercial involving a celebrity endorsement. A second randomly selected group of 75 people was shown the same TV commercial, but involving an unknown actress rather than the celebrity. Each of the 200 people was asked to rate on a scale from 0 (not persuaded) to 20 (totally persuaded) the effect on them of the commercial. A summary of the scores is shown below.

	With celebrity	Without celebrity
Sum of scores	1275	705
S_{xx}	3480	3078

Explain why the sample variances may be used as accurate estimates of the corresponding population variances.

Hence investigate the claim that the celebrity endorsement of this particular TV commercial increases its mean persuasiveness score.

Why were no distributional assumptions necessary in carrying out your test?

13 A biologist weighs each individual mouse in a random sample consisting of ten mice and records each weight to the nearest gram. The mice are then fed on a special diet and after 15 days each mouse is weighed again and the weight to the nearest gram is recorded. The results are as follows.

Initial weight (x)	50	49	48	52	40	43	51	46	41	42
Weight after 15 days (y)	52	50	50	55	42	45	52	48	42	44

Assuming that the results are given in random order on both occasions:

(a) test the hypothesis that $\sigma_x^2 = \sigma_y^2$, where σ_x^2 and σ_y^2 are the variances of the populations from which these data are taken,

(b) examine the possibility that there has been a significant increase in mean weight over the 15 days.

14 Samples are taken from two batches of paint and the viscosity, x P, measured. The information is summarised below.

Paint	Mean	Standard deviation, s	Size
A	114.44	0.62	4
B	114.93	0.94	6

Assuming normal distributions, investigate, at the 5% significance level, whether:

(a) the mean viscosity of Paint A is more than 114,

(b) the standard deviations of the viscosities of the two paints are equal,

(c) the mean viscosities of the two paints are equal.   [A]

15 The development engineer of a company making razors records the time it takes him to shave on seven mornings using a standard razor made by the company. The times, in seconds, were

217   210   254   237   232   228   243.

He wishes to compare the time taken by different designs of razor. He decides that, rather than test all the designs himself, it would be quicker to find other employees who would be willing to test one design each. As a preliminary step his assistant agrees to test the standard razor and produces the following times:

186   219   168   202   191   184

Regarding the samples as coming from normal distributions:

(a) show that there is no significant evidence of a difference between variances,

(b) test whether the mean shaving times of the engineer and his assistant are the same.

Advise the engineer how to proceed with his investigation.

[A]

16 (a) State under what circumstances you should use a pooled estimate of variance when testing for a difference between the means of two samples.

(b) During a study of the seasonal influences of Amazon river water on biological production in the western tropical Atlantic, readings were taken of the percentage water salinity during the winter and also during the summer. The following summarised data were recorded.

Period	Sample size	Sample mean	Sample standard deviation, s
Winter	96	33.60	0.816
Summer	78	33.56	0.876

It was then realised that the readings for winter were incorrect due to an error in calibration. In order to correct this error it was necessary to apply the following transformation.

Correct value = (Recorded value/0.96) − 1.23

The original readings were not available.

(i) show, by appropriate corrections to the summarised data, that the sample mean and standard deviation for winter should be 33.77 and 0.850, respectively.

(ii) Hence show that there is no evidence of a difference between the mean percentage water salinity in winter and summer for this area of the Atlantic.

(iii) State why it was **not** necessary to make any assumptions about the distributions of percentage water salinity. [A]

17 Two brands of hand cream, A and B, are sold in containers with contents of nominal volume 500 ml.

Measuring the contents of a random sample of 12 brand A containers produced a mean of 510.4 ml and an unbiased estimate of the population variance of 15.21 ml^2.

From a random sample of 20 brand B containers, the corresponding values produced were 507.8 ml and 6.76 ml^2.

The contents of each brand's containers may be assumed to have volumes that are normally distributed.

Test, at the 5% level of significance, the hypothesis that there is no difference in:

(a) the variability of content between the two brands,

(b) the mean content between the two brands. [A]

18 As part of a comparison of two brands of tea bags, A and B, one feature of interest was the weight of tea per bag.

To investigate possible differences, analyst P measured the weight, x g, of the contents of each bag in a random sample of 12 brand A tea bags with the following results:

3.45	3.55	3.70	3.75	3.32	3.20	$\bar{x} = 3.52$
3.16	3.60	3.72	3.30	3.67	3.82	$s_x = 0.2277$

A second analyst, Q, measured the weight, y g, of the contents of each bag in a random sample of 12 brand B tea bags and recorded results as follows:

3.46	3.31	3.13	3.70	3.73	3.10	$\bar{y} = 3.44$
3.45	3.40	3.78	3.39	3.45	3.38	$s_y = 0.2141$

(a) Suggest a possible source of bias in the collection of these data and indicate how it could have been avoided.

Having established that weights were approximately normally distributed, a statistician stated that it was valid to calculate a pooled estimate of variance without first carrying out the appropriate hypothesis test.

(b) Indicate why the statistician's statement appears reasonable. [You are **not** required to perform the test.]

(c) Show that, at the 5% significance level, there is no reason to disagree with the belief that the mean weight of tea per bag is the same for the two brands.

Later it transpired that the scales used by analyst Q were zeroed incorrectly. This had the effect of making each of the recorded weights for brand B tea bags 0.25 g too large.

The statistician claimed that this would make no difference to the valid use of a pooled estimate of variance nor to the conclusions regarding the mean weight of tea per bag.

(d) Determine whether or not these claims are correct.   [A]

Key point summary

I To test hypotheses about the equality of two normal population variances, or standard deviations, use   *p 56*

$$\frac{s_x^2}{s_y^2} \sim F_{n_x - 1, n_y - 1}$$

and adopt the convention of always putting the larger s^2 in the numerator.

2 To test hypotheses about the equality of (or given *p* 60 difference in) two normal population means, based upon independent random samples and known population variances, use

$$\frac{(\overline{X} - \overline{Y}) - (\mu_x - \mu_y)}{\sqrt{\dfrac{\sigma_x^2}{n_x} + \dfrac{\sigma_y^2}{n_y}}} \sim N(0, 1).$$

Note that for $n_x > 30$ and $n_y > 30$, the requirement for normal populations can be relaxed and/or sample variances can be used as estimates of population variances.

3 To test hypotheses about the equality of (or given *p* 65 difference in) two normal population means, based upon independent random samples and unknown but equal population variances, use

$$\frac{(\overline{X} - \overline{Y}) - (\mu_x - \mu_y)}{\sqrt{s_p^2 \left(\dfrac{1}{n_x} + \dfrac{1}{n_y} \right)}} \sim t_{n_x + n_y - 2}$$

where

$$s_p^2 = \frac{(n_x - 1)s_x^2 + (n_y - 1)s_y^2}{n_x + n_y - 2}.$$

Test yourself	**What to review**

1 Two newly discovered ferns, *A* and *B*, are thought to belong to *Section 5.2* the same species. Leaf length measurements were made on each fern with the following results:

Fern	Number of leaves sampled	Variance estimates, s^2 (cm²)
A	20	0.50
B	16	1.52

Stating the necessary distributional assumption, test, at the 5% level of significance, whether the population variances of leaf length are the same for the two ferns.

Section 5.3

2 The stock manager of a mail-order firm wishes to purchase a bulk supply of manila envelopes suitable for the distribution of catalogues. Firm *A* has been used in the past with satisfactory results, but a second firm, *B*, can also supply the envelopes. The stock manager will only change supplier if the envelopes from firm *B* have a greater tearing weight, on average, than those from firm *A*. Random samples of envelopes from each firm are obtained, and the tearing weight, in kilograms, is measured for each envelope by a standard test. The results are summarised below.

	Sample size	Sum of tearing weights	S_{xx}
Firm *A*	120	3540	238
Firm *B*	100	2990	297

By carrying out a suitable significance test at the 5% level, decide, on the basis of this information, whether the stock manager should change supplier.

Section 5.4

3 Mrs Chatter is a statistician and the mother of two daughters, Angela and Belinda. She suspects that the durations, *x* minutes, of telephone calls made by Angela to her friend Lucy are, on average, longer than the durations, *y* minutes, of those made by Belinda to her friend Mara.

To check this suspicion, she decides to measure the durations of independent random samples of telephone calls made by her two daughters.

The results are as follows:

Angela	13.4	16.8	12.2	13.6	10.0	$\bar{x} = 13.2$	$s_x^2 = 6.1$
Belinda	14.2	9.8	8.6	13.4	10.0	$\bar{y} = 11.2$	$s_y^2 = 6.0$

(a) Indicate why a pooled estimate of variance can be calculated without the need to first carry out the appropriate hypothesis test.

For each of Mrs Chatter's daughters, the durations of telephone calls made to her friend may be assumed to be normally distributed.

(b) Stating null and alternative hypotheses and using the 5% level of significance, investigate Mrs Chatter's suspicion.

5

Test yourself (continued)	**What to review**

<table>
<tr><td>

4 One of the questions addressed as part of an investigation into the problems of adolescence was 'Do boys worry more than girls?'

Following personal interviews, a score, based on the 'Worries Scale', was assigned to each adolescent in independent random samples of 16 boys and 12 girls. A summary of these scores is tabled below. (High scores indicate a high level of worry.)

</td><td>

Sections 5.2 and 5.4

</td></tr>
</table>

	$\bar{x}$	s^2
Boys	69.2	54.37
Girls	60.3	37.28

Scores based on the 'Worries Scale' may be assumed to be normally distributed.

(a) Show that there is no significant evidence of a difference between the variability of scores for adolescent boys and that for adolescent girls.

(b) Hence test, at the 10% level of significance, the hypothesis that boys' scores are, on average, five more than girls' scores.

Test yourself ANSWERS

1 Leaf length measurements are normally distributed, $F = 3.04$, c.v. 2.63, accept variances equal.

2 $\bar{x}_A = 29.5$, $\bar{x}_B = 29.9$, $s_A^2 = 2.0$, $s_B^2 = 3.0$, $z = 1.85$, c.v. 1.64, change supplier.

3 (a) $s_x^2 \approx s_y^2$; **(b)** $t = 1.29$, c.v. 1.86, accept means equal.

4 (a) $F = 1.46$, c.v. (5%) 3.33; **(b)** $t = 1.49$, c.v. ∓ 1.71, accept boys on average five more than girls.

CHAPTER 6

Testing for goodness of fit

Learning objectives

After studying this chapter you should be able to:

- identify conditions where the χ^2-distribution may be used for testing goodness of fit
- apply goodness of fit tests to discrete distributions
- apply goodness of fit tests to continuous distributions
- derive the appropriate degrees of freedom for goodness of fit tests.

6.1 Introduction

In chapter 5 of S4, the statistic $\sum (O - E)^2 / E$ was used to analyse contingency tables. This statistic may be used in a similar way to test the hypothesis that a set of data is a random sample from a particular distribution. The conditions under which $\sum (O - E)^2 / E$ may be approximated by the χ^2-distribution are the same as for contingency tables.

- The Os must be frequencies,
- the Es must be reasonably large, say >5,
- the classes into which the data is grouped must form a sample space – that is, every possible item of data must fit into one, and only one, class.

> $\sum (O - E)^2 / E$ may be approximated by a χ^2-distribution provided that
>
> - the Os are frequencies,
> - the Es are at least five,
> - the classes form a sample space – that is, every possible observation fits into one and only one class.

The degrees of freedom of the appropriate χ^2-distribution is the number of classes minus the number of independent pieces of information derived from the Os in order to calculate the Es. This rule is best understood by observing its application in the worked examples.

> The number of degrees of freedom is the number of classes minus the number of independent pieces of information derived from the Os in order to calculate the Es.

6.2 Goodness of fit for discrete distributions

The population of a particular country is known to have blood types O, A, B and AB in the ratio $49:38:9:4$. A medical research team, investigating an isolated community on a neighbouring island, tested a random sample of 170 individuals from this community and found the following distribution of blood types.

Blood type	O	A	B	AB
Frequency	87	59	20	4

To test the hypothesis that the blood types of the isolated community are in the same ratio as in the neighbouring country first calculate the number of each blood type expected in the sample.

If the hypothesis is true, 49% of the community are of Type O and so you would expect $0.49 \times 170 = 83.30$ Type O in the sample. Similarly you would expect

> The expected number is the long run average and so will not usually be a natural number.

$$0.38 \times 170 = 64.60 \text{ Type A}$$
$$0.09 \times 170 = 15.30 \text{ Type B}$$
$$\text{and} \quad 0.04 \times 170 = 6.80 \text{ Type AB}$$

The following table shows the observed number, O, on the left-hand side of each cell and the expected number, E, on the right-hand side of each cell.

O		A		B		AB	
87	83.30	59	64.60	20	15.30	4	6.80

$$\sum (O - E)^2/E = 3.7^2/83.3 + 5.6^2/64.6 + 4.7^2/15.3 + 2.8^2/6.8 = 3.25$$

Since the Os are frequencies, the Es are all greater than five and all possible blood types are included, $\sum (O - E)^2/E$ may be approximated by a χ^2-distribution. To find the appropriate degrees of freedom first note that there are four classes. Now you need to examine how the expected values were calculated. They were all found by multiplying 170 by a proportion (0.49, 0.38, 0.09 or 0.04) which was specified in the null hypothesis. Thus the only piece of data required from the Os in order to calculate the Es is the sample size, i.e. 170. The appropriate number of degrees of freedom is therefore $4 - 1 = 3$.

> The null hypothesis will only be rejected if $\sum (O - E)^2/E$ is large. Hence the test will be one-tailed.

For a 5% significance level the appropriate critical value is 7.815.

Hence accept the hypothesis that the distribution of blood types is the same in the isolated community as in the neighbouring country.

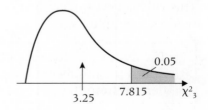

Worked example 6.1

The number of accidents per day on a stretch of motorway was recorded for 100 days and the following results obtained.

Number of accidents	0	1	2	3	4
Frequency	44	29	9	10	8

Examine whether or not a Poisson distribution is a suitable model for the number of accidents per day on this stretch of motorway. Use a 1% level of significance.

Solution

Null hypothesis H_0: the data is a random sample from a Poisson distribution.

Alternative hypothesis H_1: the data is not a random sample from a Poisson distribution.

The data gives the observed number of days on which no accidents happened. We now need to calculate how many days we would expect no accidents to happen if the data was a random sample from a Poisson distribution. To do this the mean of the distribution must be known. As this is not specified in the null hypothesis, we use the same mean as the observed data. Entering this data into a calculator a mean of 1.09 is obtained.

> Don't forget to enter the frequencies as well as the number of accidents.

The probability of no accidents on a particular day if the number of accidents follows a Poisson distribution with mean 1.09 is $e^{-1.09} = 0.3362$.

If 100 days are observed the expected number of accidents is

$$100 \times 0.3362 = 33.62.$$

Similarly the expected number of days on which any other number of accidents are observed can be calculated.

Number of accidents	$P(R = r)$	E
0	$e^{-1.09} = 0.3362$	33.62
1	$1.09e^{-1.09} = 0.3665$	36.65
2	$1.09^2 e^{-1.09}/2! = 0.1997$	19.97
3	$1.09^3 e^{-1.09}/3! = 0.0726$	7.26
4	$1.09^4 e^{-1.09}/4! = 0.0198$	1.98

> Using E to 2 decimal places should be sufficiently accurate for all questions. Do **not** round the Es to a natural number.

The largest number of accidents observed on a single day was four. However, if the data follows a Poisson distribution it would be possible for five, six or even more accidents to occur on a particular day. For the χ^2-test to be valid every possible outcome must fit into one of the classes. Hence the last class will need to be of the form 'r or more'. Bearing in mind that to apply the χ^2-test the expected numbers should be at least five, it is appropriate to make the last class '3 or more'.

> The more classes are used the smaller the risk of a Type 2 error (i.e. of accepting a false H_0). The risk of a Type 1 error (i.e. of rejecting a true H_0) is not affected by the number of classes.

The probability of 3 or more is

$$1 - 0.3362 - 0.3665 - 0.1997 = 0.0976.$$

The following table showing observed numbers on the left-hand side and expected numbers on the right-hand side, of the cells, can now be drawn up.

Number of accidents			
0	1	2	3 or more
44 33.62	29 36.65	9 19.97	18 9.76

$$\sum (O - E)^2/E = 10.38^2/33.62 + 7.65^2/36.65 + 10.97^2/19.97$$
$$+ 8.24^2/9.76 = 17.8$$

The conditions for approximating $\sum (O - E)^2/E$ by a χ^2-distribution are met – that is, the Os are frequencies, the Es are all greater than five and the classes form a sample space. There are four classes. The mean of the fitted Poisson distribution was calculated from the observed data and the Es were calculated by multiplying the probabilities by the total number of days observed. Hence there were two independent pieces of information derived from the Os in order to calculate the Es. The degrees of freedom are therefore $4 - 2 = 2$.

Sometimes H_0 may specify the mean of the Poisson distribution to be fitted. In this case there will be one more degree of freedom, as one less piece of information will be derived from the Os.

> If there are k classes and any necessary parameters are estimated from the data the number of degrees of freedom for a Poisson fit is $k - 2$.

For a 1% risk the critical value of χ^2 is 9.210.

The null hypothesis is rejected and we conclude that the data did not come from a Poisson distribution.

What interpretation can be given to this result?

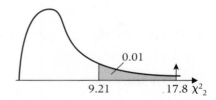

The Poisson distribution is the distribution of events which occur independently, at random, at a constant average rate. It seems that accidents did not follow this pattern – perhaps accidents were more likely to happen on days when the weather was bad and so the average rate was not constant.

Worked example 6.2

During hockey practice, each member of a squad of 60 players attempted to hit a ball between two posts. Each player had eight attempts and the numbers of successes were as follows:

```
3  4  8  1  0  3  3  4  4  2  6  7  3  2  2  5  5
5  8  1  3  5  6  1  3  4  4  4  1  0  5  3  6  0
6  7  4  3  5  7  0  1  2  6  1  8  0  0  3  0  4
4  1  3  5  0  8  1  8  8
```

(a) Use the χ^2-distribution, at the 5% significance level, to test whether the binomial distribution is an adequate model for the data.

(b) State, giving a reason, whether the data support the view that the probability of success is the same for each player.

Solution

(a) In order to apply a goodness of fit test the data must be formed into a frequency distribution.

Number of successes	0	1	2	3	4	5	6	7	8
Frequency	8	8	4	10	9	7	5	3	6

Null hypothesis H_0: the data is a random sample from a binomial distribution.

Alternative hypothesis H_1: the data is not a random sample from a binomial distribution.

First a binomial distribution must be fitted. Since each player had eight attempts, we know that n = 8. Since p is not specified in the null hypothesis a value for p will have to be obtained from the observed data.

The total number of successes is

$$(8 \times 0) + (8 \times 1) + (4 \times 2) + (10 \times 3) + (9 \times 4) + (7 \times 5)$$
$$+ (5 \times 6) + (3 \times 7) + (6 \times 8) = 216.$$

Since 60 players each had eight attempts the total number of attempts was $60 \times 8 = 480$.

The proportion of successful attempts was $216/480 = 0.45$.

Binomial probabilities can be calculated or, in the case of B(8, 0.45), found from tables.

The expected numbers are found by multiplying the probabilities by 60, the total number of players.

Number of successes	O	Probability	E
0	8	0.0084	0.504
1	8	0.0548	3.288
2	4	0.1569	9.414
3	10	0.2569	15.414
4	9	0.2626	15.756
5	7	0.1719	10.314
6	5	0.0704	4.224
7	3	0.0164	0.984
8	6	0.0017	0.102

For example, using tables

P(2) =
P(2 or fewer) – P(1 or fewer)
= 0.2201 – 0.0632 = 0.1569

Alternatively,

$P(2) = \binom{8}{2} \times 0.45^2 \times 0.55^6$
= 0.1569

In order to obtain Es which are greater than five some classes will have to be combined. As with contingency tables the most similar classes – in this case neighbouring classes – should be combined. Combining 0, 1, 2 and 6, 7, 8 is appropriate.

Number of successes	O	E
0, 1, 2	20	13.21
3	10	15.41
4	9	15.76
5	7	10.31
6, 7, 8	14	5.31

$$\sum (O - E)^2/E = 23.6$$

The conditions for approximating $\sum (O - E)^2/E$ by a χ^2-distribution are met – that is, the Os are frequencies, the Es are at least five and the classes form a sample space.

There are five classes. To calculate the Es the value of p was derived from the data and the probability of each outcome was multiplied by the total number of players. Thus two independent pieces of information were derived from the Os in order to calculate the Es. Hence there are $5 - 2 = 3$ degrees of freedom.

> If there are k classes and any necessary parameters are estimated from the data the number of degrees of freedom for a binomial fit is $k - 2$.

The critical value of χ^2 for a 5% significance level is 7.815 and so the hypothesis that the data comes from a binomial distribution is rejected.

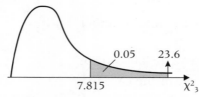

(b) For a binomial distribution the probability of success must be the same for all trials. As it is likely that different members of the squad will have different skill levels and hence different probabilities of successfully hitting the ball between the two posts it is not surprising that the data does not fit a binomial distribution.

The data does not support the view that the probability of success is the same for each player.

EXERCISE 6A

1 The owner of a small country inn observes that during the holiday season the demand for rooms is as follows:

Rooms required	0	1	2	3	4	5	6	7	8
Number of nights	2	9	16	26	33	25	20	11	5

Calculate the mean demand for rooms per night. Use a χ^2-test with a 5% significance level to determine whether the Poisson distribution is an adequate model for the data.

2 A darts player repeatedly throws three darts at a board. The number of darts from each set of three which hit the bull's-eye is summarised in the following table:

Number of bull's-eyes	0	1	2	3
Frequency	36	29	16	9

Test whether the binomial distribution provides a suitable model for this data. Use a 5% significance level.

3 Cartons of a particular brand of mixed nuts contain five different types. It is claimed that the percentages of nuts of types *A*, *B*, *C*, *D* and *E* are 35, 25, 20, 10 and 10, respectively.

A randomly selected carton is found to contain the following numbers of nuts of each type.

Type of nut	*A*	*B*	*C*	*D*	*E*
Number	184	145	100	68	63

(a) Test the hypothesis that the numbers of nuts of the different types in this carton are consistent with the claim.

(b) If a random sample of only 40 nuts had been selected, what problem would have arisen in carrying out the test? Indicate how you would deal with this problem.

[A]

4 Ninety students take a multiple choice test consisting of five questions. The number of correct answers is summarised in the table below:

Number of correct answers	0	1	2	3	4	5
Number of students	1	4	9	27	33	16

Investigate, using the 5% significance level, whether the binomial distribution provides an adequate model for the data.

Comment on the suggestion that all the students had a similar chance of answering each question correctly.

5 A college office stocks statistical tables and various items of stationery for sale to students. An analysis of the sales of statistical tables on the 130 working days of the autumn and spring terms gave the following results:

Number of statistical tables sold	0	1	2	3	4	5	6	7	8	9
Number of days		46	32	12	6	5	16	9	0	4	0

Test, at the 1% significance level, whether the Poisson distribution provides a suitable model for the data. [A]

6 The table below shows the daily opening hours of a supermarket, together with the daily numbers of customers served during a randomly chosen week.

Day	Mon	Tue	Wed	Thu	Fri	Sat	Sun
Opening hours	9	9	9	12	14	11	6
Customers	439	468	437	621	684	575	276

Use a χ^2 goodness of fit test, at the 5% level of significance, to test whether the average number of customers served per opening hour is constant throughout the week. [A]

7 The following table shows the number of male piglets born in 300 litters of size 7.

Number of males	0	1	2	3	4	5	6	7
Number of litters	0	17	54	95	80	41	12	1

Test, at the 5% level of significance, whether or not the binomial distribution with parameters n = 7, p = 0.5 is an adequate model for these data.

8 A geography student divides a map of a rural area into squares with sides representing 5 km. He counts the number of public telephones shown in each of 70 such squares and obtains the following data:

```
0  0  1  0  1  1  2  0  4  0  0  0  0  0
1  6  0  0  1  0  0  3  1  0  0  1  1  1
2  0  2  1  1  0  0  1  4  3  0  0  0  0
2  2  0  5  0  0  0  0  0  0  0  0  1  0
2  0  3  4  0  0  0  1  2  4  0  3  1  1
```

(a) Test at the 5% significance level whether the Poisson distribution provides an adequate model for the data.

(b) Does your answer support the view that public telephones in rural areas are distributed at random? [A]

9 The age distribution of respondents to a survey carried out among women shopping in Manchester city centre is shown below.

Age in years	14–17	18–24	25–39	40–60	over 60
Number of respondents	74	159	142	113	79

The percentages of women living in the Manchester area in the age groups specified are respectively 7, 13, 25, 27 and 28 (all females under 14 have been excluded).

Use a χ^2-test and a 5% significance level to test whether the age distribution of the women included in the survey is consistent with that of women living in the Manchester area. [A]

10 A factory operates four production lines. Maintenance records show that the daily number of stoppages due to mechanical failure were as follows (it is possible for a production line to break down more than once on the same day):

Number of stoppages	Number of days
0	728
1	447
2	138
3	48
4	26
5	13

(a) Use a χ^2-distribution and a 1% significance level to determine whether the Poisson distribution is an adequate model for the data.

(b) The maintenance engineer claims that breakdowns occur at random and that the mean rate has remained constant throughout the period. State, giving a reason, whether your answer to **(a)** is consistent with this claim. [A]

6.3 Goodness of fit for continuous distributions

For a continuous random variable, it is not possible to list all the different values it may take. To test for goodness of fit it is necessary to divide the possible values into classes. These classes must form a sample space – that is, every possible value of the variable must fit into one, and only one, of the classes. To test using the χ^2-distribution it may be necessary to combine these classes so that the expected values are at least 5.

Worked example 6.3

The following table summarises the waiting times, in minutes, of a random sample of 200 people at a taxi rank.

Waiting time	0–	0.5–	1.0–	1.5–2.5
Number of people	77	60	35	28

Test, using the 10% significance level, the claim that the waiting time, X, can be modelled by the probability density function

$$f(x) = \begin{cases} 0.8 - 0.32x & 0 < x < 2.5 \\ 0 & \text{otherwise.} \end{cases}$$

This is one of several possible ways of showing the classes. The class '0.5–' includes all times between 0.5 and 1.0. As the variable is continuous it makes no difference, in theory, whether or not the boundaries 0.5 and 1.0 are included.

Solution

The probability that X lies in the class 1.5 to 2.5 can be found by evaluating $\int_{1.5}^{2.5} (0.8 - 0.32x)\,dx$. Similarly the probability of X lying in the other classes may be found. The amount of work can be reduced if we first find the probability that X is less than c,

$$P(X < c) = \int_0^c (0.8 - 0.32x)\,dx = [0.8x - 0.16x^2]_0^c$$
$$= 0.8c - 0.16c^2$$

By substituting appropriate values of c, the following table can be derived.

$P(X < 0.5) = 0.36$	$P(0.0 < X < 0.5) = 0.36$
$P(X < 1.0) = 0.64$	$P(0.5 < X < 1.0) = 0.64 - 0.36 = 0.28$
$P(X < 1.5) = 0.84$	$P(1.0 < X < 1.5) = 0.84 - 0.64 = 0.20$
$P(X < 2.5) = 1.00$	$P(1.5 < X < 2.5) = 1.00 - 0.84 = 0.16$

For example, substituting $c = 0.5$ gives
$P(X < 0.5)$
$= 0.8 \times 0.5 - 0.16 \times 0.5^2$
$= 0.36$

Two hundred waiting times were observed and so the Es are the probabilities multiplied by 200.

Class	O	Probability	E
0.0–	77	0.36	72
0.5–	60	0.28	56
1.0–	35	0.20	40
1.5–2.5	28	0.16	32

The conditions for approximating $\sum (O - E)^2/E$ by a χ^2-distribution are met – that is, the Os are frequencies, the Es are at least five and the classes form a sample space.

H_0: The data is a random sample from the given probability distribution.
H_1: The data is not a random sample from the given probability distribution.

$$\sum (O - E)^2/E = 1.76$$

There are 4 classes. The only piece of information derived from the Os in order to calculate the Es was the total number of waiting times, 200. Hence there are $4 - 1 = 3$ degrees of freedom.

For a 10% significance level, the critical value is 6.251.

H_0 is accepted and we conclude that the waiting times can be modelled by the suggested probability density function.

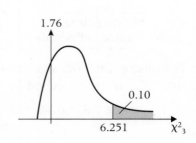

Worked example 6.4

The table below shows the time intervals, in seconds, between successive white cars in free-flowing traffic on an open road. Investigate, using the 5% significance level, whether these times can be modelled by an exponential distribution?

Time	0–	20–	40–	60–	90–	120–180
Frequency	41	19	16	13	9	2

Solution

The probability density function of an exponential distribution is

$$f(x) = \begin{cases} \lambda e^{-\lambda x} & 0 < x \\ 0 & \text{otherwise.} \end{cases}$$

The mean is $1/\lambda$.

> You have already fitted an exponential distribution in section 2.3.

The parameter λ of the exponential distribution to be fitted is not known and so the sample mean will be used as an estimate of $1/\lambda$.

Entering the class midpoints, 10, 30, 50, 75, 105 and 150, and the frequencies, into a calculator gives a mean of 40. Hence a value of $1/40 = 0.025$ is used for λ.

The probabilities of observations lying in each class can be found directly by integration but it is simpler to use the fact that the probability that X is less than c is given by

$$P(X < c) = 1 - e^{-\lambda c} = 1 - e^{-0.025c}.$$

By substituting appropriate values for c the following table can be derived.

$P(X < 20) = 0.3935$	$P(0 < X < 20) = 0.3935$
$P(X < 40) = 0.6321$	$P(20 < X < 40) = 0.6321 - 0.3935 = 0.2386$
$P(X < 60) = 0.7769$	$P(40 < X < 60) = 0.7769 - 0.6321 = 0.1448$
$P(X < 90) = 0.8946$	$P(60 < X < 90) = 0.8946 - 0.7769 = 0.1177$
$P(X < 120) = 0.9502$	$P(90 < X < 120) = 0.9502 - 0.8946 = 0.0556$
$P(X < 180) = 0.9889$	$P(120 < X < 180) = 0.9889 - 0.9502 = 0.0387$
$P(X < \infty) = 1.0000$	$P(180 < X < \infty) = 1.0000 - 0.9889 = 0.0111$

> For example, if $c = 40$
> $P(X < 40) = 1 - e^{-0.025 \times 40}$
> $\qquad = 1 - e^{-1} = 0.6321$

The Es may now be found by multiplying the probabilities by the total number of intervals observed.

That is, by $41 + 19 + 16 + 13 + 9 + 2 = 100$.

Class	O	Probability	E
0–	41	0.3935	39.35
20–	19	0.2386	23.86
40–	16	0.1448	14.48
60–	13	0.1177	11.77
90–	9	0.0556	5.56
120–	2	0.0387	3.87
180–∞	0	0.0111	1.11

The Os are frequencies and the classes form a sample space. In order to meet all the conditions for approximating $\sum (O - E)^2/E$ by a χ^2-distribution it is necessary to combine the last two classes to make the Es at least 5.

Class	O	E
0–	41	39.35
20–	19	23.86
40–	16	14.48
60–	13	11.77
90–	9	5.56
120–∞	2	4.98

In fact the E for the last class is only 4.98. As 'at least 5' is only a rule of thumb, 4.98 is acceptable. The alternative would be to make the last class 90–∞. This would reduce the degrees of freedom and increase the chance of a Type 2 error.

H_0: The time intervals may be modelled by an exponential distribution.
H_1: The time intervals may not be modelled by an exponential distribution.

$$\sum (O - E)^2/E = 5.26$$

Six classes were included in the calculation of $\sum (O - E)^2/E$. In order to calculate the Es, the total number (100) of time intervals was needed and λ was estimated from the observed values. Hence there are $6 - 2 = 4$ degrees of freedom.

> If there are k classes and any necessary parameters are estimated from the data the number of degrees of freedom when an exponential distribution is fitted is $k - 2$.

The critical value of χ^2, for the 5% significance level, is 9.488. Hence H_0 is accepted and we conclude that the exponential distribution does provide an appropriate model for the time intervals between successive white cars.

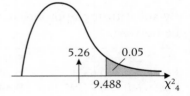

Worked example 6.5

The following table summarises the percentage fat content of a random sample of 175 hamburgers.

Fat content	Number of hamburgers
26–28	7
28–30	22
30–32	36
32–34	45
34–36	33
36–38	28
38–40	4

Can it be assumed that the fat content of this population of hamburgers is normally distributed?

Solution

First the probability of the fat content of a hamburger being in each class, if the population is normally distributed, must be calculated. To do this it is necessary to know the mean and standard deviation. As these are not given the mean and standard deviation of the observed data must be used.

Entering the class midpoints of 27, 29, 31, 33, 35, 37 and 39, together with the appropriate frequencies, into a calculator gives a mean of 33.00 and a standard deviation of 2.909.

> The divisor $n - 1$ is used for the standard deviation, s.

By standardising the class boundaries and using tables of the normal distribution the table below can be derived.

The first column headed x contains the class boundaries. Note that although there were no observations outside the range 26 to 40, it is necessary for the classes to cover all **possible** values.

The column headed z contains the class boundaries in standard form. That is $z = (x - 33)/2.909$.

The column headed $P(<z)$ is found from normal tables. Interpolation has been used but usually a sufficiently accurate answer could be found by rounding the z values to 2 decimal places.

x	z	$P(<z)$	
$-\infty$	$-\infty$	0.0000	
26	-2.407	0.0080	$P(X < 26) = 0.0080$
28	-1.719	0.0428	$P(26 < X < 28) = 0.0428 - 0.0080 = 0.0348$
30	-1.031	0.1513	$P(28 < X < 30) = 0.1513 - 0.0428 = 0.1085$
32	-0.344	0.3654	$P(30 < X < 32) = 0.3654 - 0.1513 = 0.2141$
34	0.344	0.6346	$P(32 < X < 34) = 0.6346 - 0.3654 = 0.2692$
36	1.031	0.8487	$P(34 < X < 36) = 0.8487 - 0.6346 = 0.2141$
38	1.719	0.9572	$P(36 < X < 38) = 0.9572 - 0.8487 = 0.1085$
40	2.407	0.9920	$P(38 < X < 40) = 0.9920 - 0.9572 = 0.0348$
∞	∞	1.0000	$P(X > 40) = 1.0000 - 0.9920 = 0.0080$

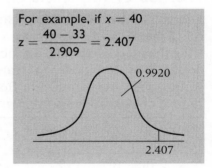

For example, if $x = 40$
$$z = \frac{40 - 33}{2.909} = 2.407$$

The expected values are found by multiplying the probabilities by 175, the total number of hamburgers in the sample. The first and last classes both have expected values of 1.4. In the following table they have been combined with their neighbours in order for all classes to have expected values greater than 5.

Class	O	Probability	E
$x < 28$	7	0.0428	7.49
$28 < x < 30$	22	0.1085	18.99
$30 < x < 32$	36	0.2141	37.47
$32 < x < 34$	45	0.2692	47.11
$34 < x < 36$	33	0.2141	37.47
$36 < x < 38$	28	0.1085	18.99
$x > 38$	4	0.0428	7.49

> The values of E are symmetrical. This is because the mean, 33.00, lies exactly in the middle of the class 32–34. This has happened by chance and will not usually be the case.

The conditions for approximating $\sum (O - E)^2/E$ by a χ^2-distribution are met – that is, the Os are frequencies, the Es are at least five and the classes form a sample space.

H_0: The percentage of fat in the population of hamburgers follows a normal distribution.
H_1: The percentage of fat in the population of hamburgers does not follow a normal distribution.

$$\sum (O - E)^2/E = 7.10$$

There are seven classes used to calculate $\sum (O - E)^2/E$. The mean and standard deviation were calculated from the Os in order to calculate the probabilities. The Es were found by multiplying the probabilities by 175, the total sample size. There are therefore $7 - 3 = 4$ degrees of freedom. The critical value of χ^2 for a 5% significance level is 9.488. H_0 is accepted and we conclude that the normal distribution provides an adequate model for the percentage of fat in the hamburgers.

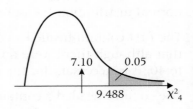

If there are k classes and any necessary parameters are estimated from the data the number of degrees of freedom when a normal distribution is fitted is $k - 3$.

Worked example 6.6

A large number of candidates sit an English examination set by a GCSE board. As part of a research exercise it was intended to scale the marks to produce a mean of 50 with a standard deviation of 10. Bhavik, a researcher, was unsure whether the scaling had been carried out. He obtained the marks of a random sample of 100 candidates and grouped the data as follows:

Mark	0–29	30–39	40–49	50–59	60–69	70–100
Frequency	5	14	24	30	17	10

Bhavik then fitted a normal distribution to the data and calculated $\sum (O - E)^2/E = 4.56$ (no classes were grouped).

(a) Test, at the 5% significance level, whether the normal distribution provides an adequate model for the data.

(b) (i) Complete the following table which shows the observed and expected values when a normal distribution with mean 50 and standard deviation 10 is fitted to the data.

Mark	$\leqslant 29$	30–39	40–49	50–59	60–69	$\geqslant 70$
O	5	14	24	30	17	10
E	2.02	12.67	33.32	34.89		

(ii) Test, at the 5% significance level, whether a normal distribution with mean 50 and standard deviation 10 provides an adequate model for the data.

(c) Summarise briefly the information you have obtained about the data and hence state whether you think it is likely that the scaling has taken place.

Solution

(a) H_0: The normal distribution provides an adequate model for the data.
H_1: The normal distribution does not provide an adequate model for the data.

There were six classes and therefore $6 - 3 = 3$ degrees of freedom when a normal distribution is fitted.

The critical value of χ^2 at the 5% significance level is 7.815.

Accept H_0 and conclude that the normal distribution provides an adequate model for the data.

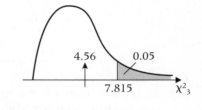

(b) (i) Since a continuous distribution is being fitted the class boundary for the last class is 69.5.

$$z = (69.5 - 50)/10 = 1.95$$

From normal tables the probability of an observation in this class is $1 - 0.974\,41 = 0.025\,59$.

The expected number in this class is $0.025\,59 \times 100 = 2.56$ to two decimal places.

The Es must total 100 and so the expected number in the class 60–69
$= 100 - 2.02 - 12.67 - 33.32 - 34.89 - 2.56 = 14.54$

The completed table is shown below.

Mark	⩽ 29	30–39	40–49	50–59	60–69	⩾ 70
O	5	14	24	30	17	10
E	2.02	12.67	33.32	34.89	14.54	2.56

(ii) H_0: The normal distribution with mean 50 and standard deviation 10 provides an adequate model for the data.
H_1: The normal distribution with mean 50 and standard deviation 10 does not provide an adequate model for the data.

To apply a χ^2-test the two end classes must be combined with their neighbours to make all Es greater than 5.

Mark	⩽ 39	40–49	50–59	⩾ 60
O	19	24	30	27
E	14.69	33.32	34.89	17.10

$$\sum (O - E)^2/E = 10.3$$

In this case the mean and standard deviation were taken from the null hypothesis and not calculated from the data. The only piece of information taken from the Os to calculate the Es was the sample size of 100. There are therefore $4 - 1 = 3$ degrees of freedom and the value of χ^2 for a test at the 5% significance level is 7.815. H_0 is rejected and we conclude that a normal distribution with mean 50 and standard deviation 10 does not provide an adequate model for the data.

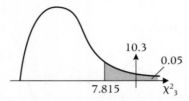

(c) It appears that the normal distribution provides an adequate model for the data but a normal distribution with mean 50 and standard deviation 10 does not. This suggests that the scaling has not taken place.

EXERCISE 6B

1 A weaving mill produces pieces of cloth. The lengths of a random sample of 150 pieces were measured. A statistician decides to check whether the lengths are normally distributed and produces the following table:

Length, m	Observed frequency	Expected frequency
<65	0	1.04
65–67	2	5.02
67–69	24	16.73
69–71	39	33.89
71–73	29	41.99
73–75	29	31.74
75–77	27	14.67
>77	0	4.92

Use the χ^2-distribution, at the 5% significance level, to test whether the normal distribution provides an adequate model for the data.

2 The table below summarises 150 random observations on the continuous random variable X.

X	0–1	1–2	2–3	3–4	4–5
Frequency	8	22	34	39	47

Test, at the 1% significance level, whether the probability density function

$$f(x) = \begin{cases} 0.08x & 0 < x < 5 \\ 0 & \text{otherwise} \end{cases}$$

provides an adequate model for X.

3 A sample of 300 electronic circuit components is selected at random from a production process. The lifetime, in hours, of each component is measured by testing it to destruction with the following summarised results:

Lifetime	0–	50–	100–	150–	200–	300–	400–	500–
Frequency	63	47	55	34	29	27	24	21

Test, at the 5% significance level, the hypothesis that the lifetimes follow an exponential distribution with mean 200 hours.

4 The nose lengths, to the nearest millimetre, of a sample of 150 adult males are summarised below.

Nose lengths (mm), x	Frequency
$x \leqslant 44$	4
$45 \leqslant x \leqslant 47$	12
$48 \leqslant x \leqslant 50$	63
$51 \leqslant x \leqslant 53$	59
$54 \leqslant x \leqslant 56$	10
$57 \leqslant x$	2

Estimate the mean and the standard deviation of the population from which these observations were taken.
(For these calculations you should assume that the first and last classes have the same width as the other classes.)

Use the χ^2-distribution and a 1% level of significance to test the adequacy of the normal distribution as a model for these data.

5 The duration, in hours, of the effect of the standard dose of a certain drug on a healthy adult female is thought to be exponentially distributed. The table below shows the results for a random sample of 200 healthy females all given the standard dose.

Duration	0–	3–	6–	9–	12–	18–	24–36
Frequency	40	31	31	22	23	22	31

Test the hypothesis that the duration of the effect is exponentially distributed. Use the 5% significance level.

6 At the end of the first year of a university course, 105 students sat an examination in statistics. The marks were grouped into classes as follows:

Mark	0–29	30–34	35–39	40–49	50–59	60–69	70–90
Number of students	6	11	4	40	26	14	4

(a) Use a χ^2-test, at the 5% significance level, to test whether the normal distribution provides an adequate model for the data.

(b) The pass mark is 40 and it is customary to review all scripts which have scored between 35 and 39 to see if it is possible to award any more marks. The marks given in the table have been subject to such a review. Comment on your results in the light of this further information and suggest how the test might be modified. [A]

7 During the production of twine, for use in the baling of hay and straw, the length, x m, between two successive faults was recorded for a period of time with the following results:

Length (x m)	Frequency
$0 < x < 100$	39
$100 < x < 200$	39
$200 < x < 300$	33
$300 < x < 500$	38
$500 < x < 1000$	37
$1000 < x < 2000$	14
$x > 2000$	0

(a) Assuming an exponential distribution, show that, correct to two decimal places, the expected frequency for '$0 < x < 100$' is 44.24. (You may assume that for an exponential distribution with mean 400,
$$P(a < X < b) = e^{-a/400} - e^{-b/400} \qquad 0 < a < b.)$$

(b) Using a χ^2 goodness of fit test and a 5% significance level, test the hypothesis that the length between two successive faults in the twine may be modelled by an exponential distribution. [A]

MIXED EXERCISE

1 A section of the accounts department of a large firm prepares invoices to send to customers. Before the invoices are sent out they are checked and the daily number of errors found over a two-week period are shown below.

	Week 1					Week 2				
	Mon	**Tue**	**Wed**	**Thu**	**Fri**	**Mon**	**Tue**	**Wed**	**Thu**	**Fri**
Errors	26	14	16	12	21	24	11	10	17	27

(a) Use the χ^2-distribution, at the 5% significance level, to test whether the data are consistent with the daily number of errors following a uniform distribution.

(b) Comment on the distribution of the errors in the light of your answer to **(a)**. [A]

2 A weaving mill sells lengths of cloth with a nominal length of 70 m. The customer measured 100 lengths and obtained the following frequency distribution:

Length (m)	Frequency
61–67	1
67–69	16
69–71	26
71–73	19
73–75	20
75–81	18

(a) Use a χ^2-test, at the 5% significance level, to show that the normal distribution is not an adequate model for the data.

(b) The contract provides for the mill to pay compensation to the customer for any lengths less than 67 m supplied. Comment on the distribution of the lengths of cloth in the light of this further information.　　　　[A]

3 A research study into complications arising from knee surgery collected data on 15 operations from each of 40 surgeons. Patients who had other serious health problems were excluded from the study. The following table summarises the number of each surgeon's patients who suffered from complications, together with the expected number when a binomial distribution is fitted to the data.

Number of patients (out of 15) with complications	0	1	2	3	4	5	6	7 or more
O	2	9	8	7	3	6	3	2
E	1.41	5.28	9.24	10.01	7.50	4.12	1.72	0.72

Test, at the 5% significance level, whether the binomial distribution is an adequate model for the data.

State, giving a reason, whether your conclusion supports the theory that the probability of a knee operation leading to complications is independent of the surgeon who carries it out.

4 A mill weaves cloth in standard lengths. When a length of cloth contains a serious blemish, the damaged section is cut out and the two remaining parts stitched together. This is known as a string. An analysis of the number of strings in 220 lengths of cloth of a particular type revealed the following data.

Number of strings	0	1	2	3	4	5	6	7
Frequency	14	29	57	48	31	41	0	0

(a) Test whether the Poisson distribution is an adequate model for the data, using a 5% significance level.

On seeing the analysis the manager pointed out that lengths of cloth containing more than five strings were unsaleable. If necessary, larger sections of cloth would be removed so that no length contained more than five strings. Without this restriction, she estimated that there would be an average of three strings per length.

If a Poisson distribution with mean 3 is fitted to the data the expected numbers are as follows:

Number of strings	0	1	2	3	4	5 or more
Expected number	10.96	32.85	49.29	49.29	36.98	40.63

(b) Test whether a Poisson distribution with mean 3 is an adequate model for the data provided all observations of five or more are classified together (as is the case in this part). Use a 5% significance level.

(c) In the light of your calculations in **(a)** and **(b)** discuss whether it is likely that serious blemishes occur at random at a constant average rate throughout the cloth.

[A]

5 As part of a statistics project, students observed five private cars passing a college and counted the number which were carrying the driver only, with no passengers. This was repeated 80 times. The results of a particular student were as follows:

Number of cars with driver only	Frequency
0	0
1	3
2	12
3	27
4	26
5	12

(a) Use the χ^2-distribution and a 5% significance level to test whether the binomial distribution provides an adequate model for the data.

In a further part of the project the students counted the number of cars passing the college in 130 intervals each of length five seconds. The following table shows the results obtained by the same student together with the expected numbers if a Poisson distribution, with the same mean as the observed data, is fitted.

Number of cars passing a point in a five second interval	0	1	2	3	4	5	6	7 or more
Number of intervals	28	40	32	19	7	3	1	0
Number of intervals expected	25.85	41.75	33.72	18.16	7.33	2.37	0.64	0.18

(b) Use the χ^2-distribution and a 5% significance level to test whether the Poisson distribution provides an adequate model for the data.

(c) The teacher suspected that this student had not observed the data but had invented them. Explain why the teacher was suspicious and comment on the strength of the evidence supporting her suspicions. [A]

6 A computer is programmed to generate integers from the set 1, 2, 3, ..., 15.

The random variable R denotes the number of integers generated to obtain an integer which is a multiple of 3.

The following probability model for R is suggested.

$$P(R = r) = p(1 - p)^{r - 1} \qquad r = 1, 2, 3, \ldots$$

where p is the probability that a generated integer is a multiple of 3. The table shows the results of 160 observations of R.

Number of integers generated (r)	1	2	3	4	5	6	7	8	>8
Frequency		63	34	28	13	9	7	2	4	0

(a) Calculate the mean, $\bar{r}$, of these data.

(b) Given that $\bar{r}$ is an estimate of $1/p$, use a χ^2 goodness of fit test, with a 5% level of significance, to test whether the suggested probability model for R is appropriate. [A]

7 A weaving mill produces pieces of cloth. The lengths of a random sample of 150 pieces were measured. The mean length was 71.867 m and the standard deviation was 2.787 m.

(a) Assume that the lengths are normally distributed and that 2.787 m is an accurate estimate of the population standard deviation.

(i) Calculate a 90% confidence interval for the mean length.

(ii) Assuming also that 71.867 m is an accurate estimate of the population mean, calculate an interval within which 90% of the lengths will lie.

A statistician decides to check the assumption that the data are normally distributed. She obtains the original data and fits a normal distribution with the following result.

Length, m	Observed frequency	Expected frequency
<65	0	1.04
65–67	2	5.02
67–69	24	16.73
69–71	39	33.89
71–73	29	41.99
73–75	29	31.74
75–77	27	14.67
>77	0	4.92

(b) Use the χ^2-distribution, at the 5% significance level, to test whether the normal distribution provides an adequate model for the data.

(c) In view of your answer to **(b)**, how reliable, in your opinion, are the results that you calculated in **(a)**? Give a reason for your answer. [A]

Key point summary

1 $\sum (O - E)^2/E$ may be approximated by a χ^2-distribution provided that   *p 79*

   - the Os are frequencies,
   - the Es are at least five,
   - the classes form a sample space – that is, every possible observation fits into one and only one class.

2 The number of degrees of freedom is the number of classes minus the number of independent pieces of information derived from the Os in order to calculate the Es.   *p 79*

3 If there are k classes and any necessary parameters are estimated from the data the number of degrees of freedom is $k - 2$ for a Poisson, binomial or exponential distribution and $k - 3$ for a normal distribution.   *p 82*   *p 84*   *p 90*   *p 92*

Test yourself   **What to review**

1 The number of batteries sold daily over a period of one hundred working days by a small garage is summarised in the following table. The table also shows the expected number of days on which 0, 1, 2, 3 or 4 batteries would be sold if the data followed a Poisson distribution.   *Section 6.2*

Batteries sold	0	1	2	3	4
O	16	26	32	14	12
E	16.52	29.76	26.78	16.06	7.24

Why is it necessary to change the last class to '4 or more' before applying a goodness of fit test?

Test yourself (*continued*)	What to review

2 If, in question 1, the last class is changed to '4 or more' find the new expected value. *Section 6.2*

3 Apply a goodness of fit test to the data in question 1. *Section 6.2*

4 Does your conclusion to question 3 support the belief that battery sales at the garage occur at random at a constant average rate? Explain your answer. *Section 6.2*

5 *Section 6.2*

Outcome	0	1	2	3	4	5 or more
Frequency	12	14	23	37	32	19

Write down the appropriate critical values for the following goodness of fit tests applied to the data above. Assume, in all cases that it is unnecessary to group classes.

(a) Poisson, mean 3, 1% significance level.
(b) Binomial, n = 8, 5% significance level.
(c) Binomial n = 10, p = 0.3, 0.5% significance level.

6 A normal distribution is fitted to a set of data consisting of nine classes. The value of $\sum (O - E^2)/E$ is 12.4. Carry out a goodness of fit test at the 5% significance level. *Section 6.3*

7 A statistician wishes to test whether the interval of time, in hours, between machine breakdowns in a workshop can be modelled by the following exponential distribution: *Section 6.3*

$$f(x) = \begin{cases} 0.04e^{-0.04x} & 0 < x \\ 0 & \text{otherwise.} \end{cases}$$

(a) If 200 observations are made calculate the expected value for the class 20–25.

(b) If the data is divided into seven classes find the critical value for carrying out a goodness of fit test at the 1% significance level.

1 For a goodness of fit test to be valid the classes must form a sample space. That is, all possible outcomes must be included in one of the classes.

2 10.88.

3 $X^2 = 1.89$, c.v. for 5% significance level 7.815. Accept sales may be modelled by a Poisson distribution.

4 Yes, Poisson distribution implies events occur at random at a constant average rate.

5 (a) 15.086; (b) 9.488; (c) 16.750.

6 c.v. 12.592 accept (just) normal is an adequate model.

7 (a) 16.3; (b) 16.812.

Testing the parameter β of the regression equation

Learning objectives

After studying this chapter you should be able to:

- test hypotheses about the value of the parameter β of the regression equation, assuming the model $Y = \alpha + \beta x + \varepsilon$, where ε is $N(0, \sigma^2)$
- understand the implications of the model you have assumed
- decide whether or not it is plausible to use this model in particular circumstances.

7.1 Introduction

Regression was introduced in chapter 9 of S1. In that chapter you studied the relationship between a response (or dependent) variable and a non-random explanatory (or predictor or independent) variable. As an example of this model the response variable could be the temperature of a room and the explanatory variable could be the time since an electric fire was switched on. As another example, the response variable could be the daily takings of a department store and the explanatory variable could be the number of sales assistants present. In both these examples the value of the explanatory variable may be chosen and the value of the response variable is then observed. In this chapter you will see how to use hypothesis testing to examine whether there is significant evidence that these variables are related.

7.2 The simple linear regression model

In some cases the relationship between two variables may appear almost exactly linear. If this is so all that is necessary is to determine the equation of the line. However, in most cases there will not be an exact linear relationship between the values of two variables. Nevertheless you may still wish to explain the relationship in terms of a linear model.

The model used is

> $$Y = \alpha + \beta x + \varepsilon$$
>
> where α and β are constants, x is a variable which may be set to any chosen value and ε is $N(0, \sigma^2)$.

Lower case x is used to indicate that the value of x may be chosen and so it is not a random variable. Upper case Y is used to indicate that Y is a random variable. Its value may be observed but cannot be chosen. (You will not be penalised for using the wrong case.)

Here ε represents experimental error – that is, the effect on Y of all factors other than x. For example, the weather and the amount spent on advertising will affect the takings of the department store as well as the number of sales assistants present. The model assumes that this experimental error is a random sample from a normal distribution with standard deviation σ. It also assumes that σ is a constant for all values of x. The model can never be proved to be 'true' but, after a line has been fitted to a set of data, an examination of the residuals can establish whether or not the model is plausible.

The mathematical development of simple linear regression is based on this model.

The following data was used in section 9.3 of S1. It shows the fuel consumption of a lorry when carrying different loads.

x lorry load (000s kg)	5.0	5.7	6.5	7.0	7.6	8.5	9.5	10.5
y fuel consumption (km l^{-1})	6.21	6.12	5.90	5.62	5.25	5.41	5.32	5.11

This data is analysed in Worked example 7.1.

The least squares regression equation $y = 7.15 - 0.203x$ can be obtained by using a calculator.

A second set of data could be collected using the same loads on the lorry, i.e. the same values of x. If the model $Y = \alpha + \beta x + \varepsilon$ applies then, although the values of x are the same, the values of Y would be different. This is because the values of the experimental errors, ε, would be different. If the regression equation is calculated for this new set of data it would not be exactly the same as the equation calculated from the first set of data, $y = 7.15 - 0.203x$.

Hence 7.15 will not be equal to α, but will be an estimate of α. Similarly -0.203 will not be equal to β but will be an estimate of β. These estimates are denoted $\hat{\alpha}$ and $\hat{\beta}$ respectively.

In S1 the equation was denoted $y = a + bx$. It is usual to use a, b when no particular model is assumed and $\hat{\alpha}$, $\hat{\beta}$ when this model is assumed.

An unlimited number of estimates $\hat{\beta}$ could be obtained and would form a distribution. It may be shown – the mathematics required is beyond (but not all that far beyond) A level – that the distribution of $\hat{\beta}$ is normal with mean β and variance $\sigma^2 / \sum (x - \bar{x})^2$. This variance may be written σ^2 / S_{xx}.

> $\hat{\beta}$ is normally distributed with mean β and variance σ^2 / S_{xx}.

The notation S_{xx} is used in the AQA formulae book.

Hence, if σ^2 were known it would be possible to test hypotheses about β.

The usual hypothesis of interest is $\beta = 0$. If this is true, then the model becomes $Y = \alpha + \varepsilon$.

The variable, x, no longer appears in the equation and so there is no evidence of a relationship between the two variables. However, if the hypothesis $\beta = 0$ is rejected, there is positive evidence of an underlying linear relationship between the two variables.

> If $\beta \neq 0$ there is positive evidence of a linear relationship between x and Y.

In practice, it is highly unlikely that the value of σ^2 will be known and so it must be estimated from the data. The equation of the model may be rearranged to give $\varepsilon = Y - \alpha - \beta x$ and so ε may be estimated by the residual $y - \hat{\alpha} - \hat{\beta}x$. Again the mathematics is a little beyond A level but it can be shown that an unbiased estimate of σ^2 is given by $\sum \varepsilon^2/(n-2) = \sum (y - \hat{\alpha} - \hat{\beta}x)^2/(n-2)$.

In the AQA formulae book $\sum (y - \hat{\alpha} - \hat{\beta}x)^2$ is denoted RSS.

This unbiased estimate of σ^2 is denoted s^2 in the AQA formulae book. This is the same as the symbol used for $\dfrac{\sum (x - \bar{x})^2}{n-1}$.
However, this should not lead to confusion as the appropriate formula for s^2 will be clear from the context.

> An unbiased estimate of σ^2 is given by
> $s^2 = \sum (y - \hat{\alpha} - \hat{\beta}x)^2/(n-2)$.

There are a number of possible ways of reducing the labour of this calculation. The AQA formulae book gives $\sum (y - \hat{\alpha} - \hat{\beta}x)^2 = S_{yy}(1 - r^2)$, where r is the product moment correlation coefficient between X and Y, and $S_{yy} = \sum (y - \bar{y})^2$. The value of r may be obtained directly using a calculator. Some calculators will also give S_{yy}. Alternatively, $S_{yy} = (n-1)s_y^2$.

The AQA formulae book gives a number of alternative formulae. Use whichever you are most comfortable with.

> $\sum (y - \hat{\alpha} - \hat{\beta}x)^2 = S_{yy}(1 - r^2)$

7.3 Testing hypotheses about β

The following data arose from an experiment carried out in an industrial research laboratory. A plastic plate was immersed in liquid and subjected to various strains. The deflection of the plate was measured. For reasons of commercial secrecy, the data are only available in coded form. In this case, the strain is the explanatory variable and the deflection is the response variable.

Strain, x	152	260	63	240	73	248	65	265	145	366	151
Deflection, y	2.79	3.38	2.26	3.25	2.31	3.23	2.26	3.28	3.10	4.34	3.15

The regression line may be found directly using a calculator to be $y = 1.94 + 0.00591x$.

Also using the calculator,

$$r = 0.950389 \quad s_x = 98.7160 \quad s_y = 0.614049$$

> The coefficients have been given to 3 s.f., but more than 3 s.f. will be used for $\hat{\beta}$ in the calculation below.

Plotting the points and superimposing the line give no reason to doubt the plausibility of the model.

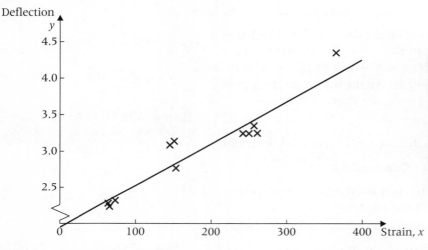

> The residual is the observed value of y minus the value predicted by the regression equation. That is, it is the vertical distance of the point from the line. Residuals can be examined by eye. In this case there are none which are much larger than the others and there is no particular pattern.

For the first point, the observed value of Y was 2.79 and the value predicted by the model is $1.94 + 0.00591 \times 152 = 2.84$. Thus the residual is $2.79 - 2.84 = -0.05$.

> If this residual was to be used for further calculations it would have been necessary to keep more than 2 d.p.

An estimate of σ^2 can be made by calculating all the residuals and then squaring and adding them. However, it is quicker to use $\sum(y - \hat{\alpha} - \hat{\beta}x)^2 = S_{yy}(1 - r^2)$.

$$S_{yy} = (n - 1)s_y^2 = (11 - 1) \times 0.614049\,1^2 = 3.770\,56$$

$$\sum(y - \hat{\alpha} - \hat{\beta}x)^2 = 3.770\,56(1 - 0.950389^2) = 0.364\,840$$

σ^2 is estimated by $\sum(y - \hat{\alpha} - \hat{\beta}x)^2/(n - 2) = 0.364\,840/(11 - 2)$
$$= 0.040\,537\,7$$

The variance of $\hat{\beta}$ is σ^2/S_{xx}.

$$S_{xx} = (n - 1)s_x^2 = (11 - 1) \times 98.7160^2 = 97\,448.545$$

An unbiased estimate of the variance of $\hat{\beta}$ is

$$0.040\,537\,7/97\,448.545 = 0.000\,000\,415\,99$$

The standard deviation of $\hat{\beta}$ is estimated by $\sqrt{0.000\,000\,415\,99}$
$$= 0.000\,644\,97$$

If $\beta = 0$ then Y and x are not related. This can now be tested.

$\quad$ H$_0$: $\beta = 0$ $\quad$ H$_1$: $\beta > 0$

The difference between our estimate of β (0.005 912) and the hypothesised value of β (0) is expressed in units of standard deviations. As the standard deviation was estimated the critical values will be obtained from the t-distribution.

$\quad t = 0.005\,912/0.000\,644\,97 = 9.2$

The estimate of standard deviation was based on $n - 2 = 9$ degrees of freedom and so the critical value for a 5% one-sided risk is 1.833 and the null hypothesis is clearly rejected (as it would be even for a 0.1% risk). There is clear evidence that the deflection is affected by the strain.

It is possible to test hypotheses other than $\beta = 0$. For example, if there had been reason to expect β to be 0.005, this could have been tested as follows:

$\quad$ H$_0$: $\beta = 0.005$ $\quad$ H$_1$: $\beta \neq 0.005$

$\quad\quad t = (0.005\,912 - 0.005)/0.000\,644\,97 = 1.41$

For a 5% two-sided risk, the critical values are ± 2.262 and the hypothesis $\beta = 0.005$ is accepted.

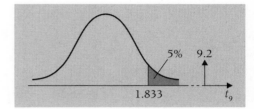

A one-tailed test is chosen as the deflection would be expected to increase as the strain increases.

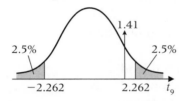

$\quad$ To test the hypothesis $\beta = \beta_0$ use $\dfrac{\beta - \beta_0}{\sqrt{S^2/S_{xx}}} \sim t_{n-2}$.

Worked example 7.1

The following table shows the fuel consumption of a lorry when carrying different loads.

This is the data introduced on page 104.

x lorry load (000s kg)	5.0	5.7	6.5	7.0	7.6	8.5	9.5	10.5
y fuel consumption (km l^{-1})	6.21	6.12	5.90	5.62	5.25	5.41	5.32	5.11

(a) Plot the data.
(b) Find the equation of the regression line of fuel consumption on load. Draw the line on your scatter diagram.
(c) Comment on the plausibility of the model $Y = \alpha + \beta x + \varepsilon$, where ε is N(0, σ^2).
(d) Test the hypothesis $\beta = 0$, using the 1% significance level.
(e) Interpret your conclusion to (d) in the context of this question.

Solution

(a)

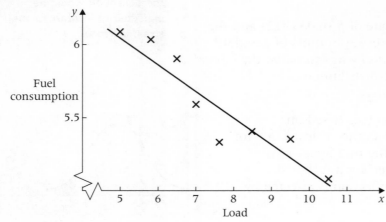

(b) The equation of the regression line is $y = 7.15 - 0.203x$ using a calculator.

Although they are not needed for this part it is worth recording here other results from the calculator which will be needed later.

$$r = -0.920\,522\,6 \quad s_x = 1.879\,922\,1 \quad s_y = 0.415\,339\,7$$

Three significant figures is adequate for stating and drawing the equation of the regression line. However for **(d)** it is desirable to record the estimate of β to more than three significant figures, i.e. $-0.203\,375$.

(c) It is likely that fuel consumption will depend on load – certainly load will not depend on fuel consumption. Hence it is appropriate to choose Y as the dependent variable.

Examining the residuals shows no particular pattern and although the fifth point has a fairly large negative residual it is not large enough to cast serious doubt on the normal model. The model is therefore plausible.

(d) $S_{yy} = (n-1)s_y^2 = (8-1) \times 0.415\,339\,7^2 = 1.207\,550$

$$\sum (y - \hat{\alpha} - \hat{\beta}x)^2 = S_{yy}(1 - r^2)$$

$$= 1.207\,55(1 - (-0.920\,522\,6)^2) = 0.184\,318\,1$$

σ^2 is estimated by
$\sum (y - \hat{\alpha} - \hat{\beta}x)^2/(n-2) = 0.184\,318\,1/(8-2)$
$$= 0.030\,719\,6$$

$S_{xx} = (n-1)s_x^2 = (8-1) \times 1.879\,922\,1^2 = 24.738\,75$

An unbiased estimate of the variance of β is
$s^2/S_{xx} = 0.030\,719\,6/24.738\,75 = 0.001\,241\,7$
$H_0: \beta = 0 \quad H_1: \beta \neq 0.$
$t = -0.203\,375/\sqrt{0.001\,241\,7} = -5.77$
Critical values of t_6 for 1% risk are ± 3.707
Reject H_0 and conclude: $\beta \neq 0.$

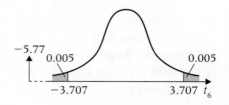

(e) There is significant evidence to suggest that as the load increases the number of kilometres covered per litre of fuel decreases.

Worked example 7.2

Cucumbers are stored in brine before being processed into pickles. It is suspected that y, a measure of the firmness of the pickles produced, is related to x, the percentage of sodium chloride in the salt used to make the brine. The value of x was deliberately varied for different batches of cucumbers and the value of y determined. The following data was collected.

x	6.0	6.5	7.0	7.5	8.0	8.5	9.0	9.5
y	15.8	15.3	16.1	16.9	16.8	17.9	16.9	17.7

$$\Sigma(y - \hat{\alpha} - \hat{\beta}x)^2 = 1.4433, \ \Sigma x = 62, \ \Sigma x^2 = 491$$

The equation of the regression line of y on x is $y = 11.8 + 0.633x$. Assume the model $Y = \alpha + \beta x + \varepsilon$; where ε is $N(0, \sigma^2)$.

(a) Plot a scatter diagram of the data. Draw the regression line on your scatter diagram.
(b) Estimate σ^2.
(c) Estimate the variance of $\hat{\beta}$, the estimated value of β.
(d) Using the 5% significance level, test the hypothesis $\beta = 0$.
(e) Explain the meaning of your conclusion in (d) in the context of this question.
(f) Comment on the plausibility, or otherwise, in this case, of the model you have been told to assume.

> In this question some intermediate results are given. This is likely to happen in examination questions as the calculation is lengthy. However, the results which are given and the form they are given in will vary.

7

Solution

(a)

(b) Estimate of $\sigma^2 = 1.4433/(8 - 2) = 0.240\,55$.

(c) Estimate of the variance of $\hat{\beta} = 0.240\,55/(491 - 62^2/8)$
$$= 0.022\,91$$

In this question $\sum x$ and $\sum x^2$ were given. In other questions S_{xx} or s_x might be given.

(d) $H_0: \beta = 0$ $H_1: \beta \neq 0$
$t = 0.633/\sqrt{0.022\,91} = 4.18$
c.v. t_6 for a 5% two-sided test ± 2.447
Reject H_0, there is significant evidence that $\beta \neq 0$.

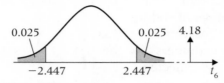

(e) There is evidence that y, the firmness of cucumber pickles, is affected by x, the percentage of sodium chloride in the brine, at least over the range of values of x used. Large percentages of sodium chloride lead to large values of y.

(f) There are no outliers and no obvious pattern to the residuals. Hence, the model $N(0, \sigma^2)$ is plausible. The firmness of the pickles is measured for predetermined values of the percentage of sodium chloride, so the model is entirely appropriate.

EXERCISE 7A

1 The variables x and Y can be modelled by $Y = \alpha + \beta x + \varepsilon$, where ε is $N(0, \sigma^2)$.

Seven paired observations have the following values:

x	16	25	37	44	50	69	80
y	23	54	76	100	138	152	183

Given that the regression equation is $y = -8.708 + 2.452x$, $\sum (y - \hat{\alpha} - \hat{\beta}x)^2 = 768.38$ and $\sum (x - \bar{x})^2 = 3126.86$:
(a) estimate σ^2,
(b) test the hypothesis $\beta = 0$. Use the 1% significance level.

2 The variables x and Y can be modelled by $Y = \hat{\alpha} + \hat{\beta}x + \varepsilon$, where ε is $N(0, \sigma^2)$.

Eight paired observations have the following values:

x	0.23	0.78	0.45	0.24	0.76	1.03	1.24	0.99
y	4.9	14.9	10.9	3.6	18.2	29.8	30.2	18.4

Given that the regression equation is $y = -1.816 + 25.42x$, $r = 0.9511$ and $S_{yy} = 705.82$:
(a) estimate σ^2,
(b) test the hypothesis $\beta = 0$. Use the 5% significance level.

3 The variables x and Y can be modelled by $Y = \alpha + \beta x + \varepsilon$, where ε is $N(0, \sigma^2)$.

Six paired observations have the following values:

x	11.2	23.8	6.4	35.2	46.3	40.9
y	5.8	3.6	6.1	2.8	1.9	1.7

Given that the regression equation is $y = 6.8044 - 0.1155x$, $r = -0.9824$, $s_x = 16.23$ and $s_y = 1.909$:

(a) estimate σ^2,

(b) test the hypothesis $\beta < 0$, using the 5% significance level.

4 The table below gives values of nine pairs of observations.

x	23	34	84	76	22	39	48	66	55
y	11	21	37	46	7	19	31	27	30

Assuming that the variables x and Y can be modelled by $Y = \alpha + \beta x + \varepsilon$, where ε is $N(0, \sigma^2)$, test the hypothesis

(a) $\beta = 0$, using the 5% significance level,

(b) $\beta = 0.5$, using the 5% significance level,

(c) $\beta < 0.9$, using the 1% significance level.

5 An electric fire was switched on in a cold room and the temperature of the room was noted at five minute intervals.

Time, minutes from switching on fire, x	0	5	10	15	20	25	30	35	40
Temperature, °C, y		0.4	1.5	3.4	5.5	7.7	9.7	11.7	13.5	15.4

$\sum (y - \hat{\alpha} - \hat{\beta}x)^2 = 0.591\,555$ and $S_{xx} = 1500$

(a) Plot the data on a scatter diagram.

(b) Find the equation of the regression line of temperature on time and draw it on your diagram.

Assuming the model $Y = \alpha + \beta x + \varepsilon$, where ε is $N(0, \sigma^2)$:

(c) estimate σ^2,

(d) use the 5% significance level to test the hypothesis $\beta = 0$,

(e) Explain why the regression line of temperature on time was used rather than the regression line of time on temperature,

(f) Comment on the plausibility of the model you have assumed. [A]

6 Technicians carry out laboratory trials to examine the effect of temperature on the yield of an industrial process. The table shows the results obtained.

x, temperature, °C	10	15	20	25	30	35	40	45	50	55	60	65
y, yield, kg		80	106	75	90	117	118	97	127	80	109	140	115

$r = 0.548\,933$ $S_{xx} = 3575$ $S_{yy} = 4575$

(a) Draw a scatter diagram of the data.

(b) Calculate the regression line of y on x and draw it on your scatter diagram.

(c) By examining the scatter diagram comment on the residuals.

Assuming the model $Y = \alpha + \beta x + \varepsilon$, where ε is $N(0, \sigma^2)$:

(d) estimate σ^2,

(e) use the 5% significance level to test the hypothesis $\beta = 0$,

(f) interpret your answers to (c) and (e) in the context of the question. [A]

7 As part of a practical exercise in statistics, Miriam was shown photographs of 11 people and asked to estimate their ages. The actual ages and the estimates made by Miriam are shown below.

Actual age, x	86	55	28	69	45	7	17	11	37	2	78
Miriam's estimate, y	88	60	35	77	50	8	15	6	49	2	85

(a) Draw a scatter diagram of Miriam's estimate, y, and the actual age, x.

(b) Calculate the equation of the regression line of Miriam's estimate on actual age and draw it on your diagram.

(c) Assuming the model $Y = \alpha + \beta x + \varepsilon$, where ε is $N(0, \sigma^2)$, test the hypothesis $\beta = 1$, using the 1% significance level.

(d) Comment on the suitability of the model you have used and interpret your conclusions. [A]

8 The following data relate to trials carried out in a laboratory to examine the relationship between the amount of a certain chemical used in a process and the concentration of the final product.

Amount, g, of chemical, x	22	24	30	32	34	36	40	42	44	46
Concentration, y		1.1	1.6	0.9	1.9	1.5	1.1	1.8	2.4	1.2	1.7

(a) Draw a scatter diagram of the data.

(b) Calculate the regression line of y on x and draw it on your scatter diagram.

(c) By examining your scatter diagram comment on the residuals.

Assuming the model $Y = \alpha + \beta x + \varepsilon$, where ε is $N(0, \sigma^2)$:

(d) estimate σ^2,

(e) use the 5% significance level to test the hypothesis $\beta = 0$,

(f) interpret your answers to (c) and (e) in the context of the question. Comment on the choice of concentration as the dependent variable and the amount of chemical as the explanatory variable. [A]

9 In addition to its full-time staff, a supermarket employs part-time sales staff on Saturdays. The manager experimented to see if there is a relationship between the takings and the number of part-time staff employed. The following data relates to nine successive Saturdays.

Part-time staff employed, x	10	13	16	19	22	25	28	31	34
Takings, £'00, y		313	320	319	326	333	342	321	361	355

$$\sum (y - \hat{\alpha} - \hat{\beta}x)^2 = 689.54 \text{ and } \sum (x - \bar{x})^2 = 540.$$

The equation of the regression line of takings on part-time staff is $y = 294 + 1.73x$.

(a) Plot the data and draw the regression line on your scatter diagram.

(b) Assuming the model $Y = \alpha + \beta x + \varepsilon$, where ε is $N(0, \sigma^2)$, use the 5% significance level to test the hypothesis $\beta = 0$.

(c) On one of the Saturdays, major roadworks blocked a nearby main road. Which Saturday do you think this was? Give a reason for your choice.

(d) In the light of the residuals and **(c)** discuss the likely validity of the model.

(e) Repeat the analysis of **(b)** leaving out the data for the Saturday when you think major roadworks took place.

(f) Discuss your overall findings. [A]

10 The bar at a sports club always opens for six hours on Saturdays when the club is busiest and the receipts per hour are highest. Other opening hours vary from week to week. The following table shows the weekly number of hours for which the bar was open and the weekly bar receipts for an eight-week period.

Hours open, x	13.0	14.0	20.5	17.0	8.5	14.5	10.0	12.0
Receipts, £, y	1364	1285	1632	1581	1102	1429	1121	1292

(a) Plot a scatter diagram of the data.

(b) Calculate the equation of a suitable regression line. Explain your choice of dependent and explanatory variables.

(c) Plot your regression line on the scatter diagram.

(d) Give an interpretation to the value of β in the context of this question.

It is estimated that it is profitable to keep the bar open provided takings exceed £40 per hour.

(e) Investigate, using a 5% significance level, whether takings, excluding the six hours on Saturday exceed £40 per hour.

(f) Interpret your conclusions in the context of this question. [A]

Key point summary

1 Hypothesis testing in the context of linear regression   *p 104*
assumes the model

$$Y = \alpha + \beta x + \varepsilon$$

where α and β are constants, x is a variable which
may be set to any chosen value and ε is $N(0, \sigma^2)$.

2 $\hat{\beta}$ is normally distributed with mean β and variance   *p 104*
σ^2/S_{xx}, where $S_{xx} = \sum (x - \bar{x})^2$.

3 An unbiased estimate of σ^2 is given by   *p 105*
$s^2 = \sum (y - \hat{\alpha} - \hat{\beta}x)^2/(n - 2)$.

4 $\sum (y - \hat{\alpha} - \hat{\beta}x)^2 = S_{yy}(1 - r^2)$.   *p 105*

5 To test the hypothesis $\beta = \beta_0$ use $\dfrac{\beta - \beta_0}{\sqrt{S^2/S_{xx}}}$.   *p 107*

6 If $\beta \neq 0$ there is positive evidence of a linear   *p 105*
relationship between x and Y.

Test yourself	What to review
1 The usual model for linear regression is $Y = \alpha + \beta x + \varepsilon$, where ε is $N(0, \sigma^2)$. Explain what this model implies about the experimental error.	*Section 7.2*
2 Athletes perform a repetitive exercise and their coach records their pulse rate after different numbers of repetitions. In a regression model which of the two variables would you choose as the dependent variable and which as the explanatory variable? Explain your answer.	*Section 7.1*
3 Twenty paired observations of pulse rate and number of repetitions are available from the exercise in Question 2. State the critical value for investigating, at the 5% significance level, whether pulse rate increases with the number of repetitions.	*Section 7.3*
4 The hypothesis $\beta = 0$ is tested for the model $Y = \alpha + \beta x + \varepsilon$, where ε is $N(0, \sigma^2)$. Explain what accepting this hypothesis implies about the relationship between Y and x.	*Section 7.3*
5 Sixteen observations on the paired variables x and Y lead to the regression equation $y = 12 - 23x$. $$S_{xx} = 196, \quad S_{yy} = 248 \quad \text{and} \quad r = -0.654.$$ Test the hypothesis $\beta = -22$ assuming the usual model and using the 5% significance level.	*Section 7.3*

Test yourself (continued)   What to review

6

x	2	4	6	8	10
y	3	5	9	7	12

Section 7.3

Find the regression line of Y on x for the data above.
Assuming the usual model, test the hypothesis $\beta = 0$ using a
1% significance level.

Test yourself   ANSWERS

1 The model assumes that experimental error may be regarded as
a random sample from a normal distribution. Also that this
distribution has the same standard deviation for all values of x.

2 Dependent variable pulse rate. This is because the number of
repetitions could affect the pulse but the pulse rate cannot
affect the numbers of repetitions.

3 1.734.

4 There is no evidence that x and Y are related.

5 $t = -4.40$, cv ± 2.145, conclude $\beta \neq -22$ (β less than -22).

6 $y = 1.2 + x$, $t = 3.69$, cv ± 5.841, accept $\beta = 0$.

Exam style practice paper

Time allowed 1 hour 15 minutes

Answer **all** questions

1 Each individual in a random sample of 40 adults was asked to identify their major source of news information. The responses showed that 25 considered that their major source was television news coverage.

Investigate, at the 5% level of significance, the claim that more than half the adult population consider television to be their major source of news information. *(4 marks)*

2 The time, X weeks, between successive breakdowns in a power supply may be modelled by the following distribution function:

$$P(X < x) = 1 - e^{-0.005x} \quad x > 0$$

(a) Find the probability that the time between successive breakdowns will be between 150 and 250 weeks. *(3 marks)*

(b) State the mean and the standard deviation of the times between successive breakdowns. *(2 marks)*

3 The number of injuries reported in a factory may be modelled by a Poisson distribution. A new safety officer was appointed who then introduced more stringent safety measures. From a random sample of 70 days, following the implementation of the new measures, 171 injuries were reported.

Use this information to investigate, at the 5% level of significance, whether the new measures have resulted in a reduction from 2.8 in the daily mean number of reported injuries. *(6 marks)*

4 In a controlled experiment to test the accuracy of an air-pump gauge, a container was inflated repeatedly to 200 Pa as recorded by the gauge. After each inflation the air pressure, x Pa, in the container was measured by an accurately calibrated device. The results of 16 independent inflations are shown below.

187	213	204	194	207	211	198	213
201	187	207	209	203	200	189	209

(a) Stating the necessary distributional assumption, calculate a 95% confidence interval for the variance of the above measurements. *(8 marks)*

(b) If regulations stipulate that the standard deviation of air-pump gauge recordings must not exceed 10 Pa, what can be concluded? *(2 marks)*

5 A retail fruiterer stocks two varieties of oranges, P and Q, for distribution to retail outlets.

Inspector A measured the weight, x g, of each of a random sample of 10 oranges of variety P with the following results:

   155   146   149   156   161   158   144   148   165   158
   $\bar{x} = 154$ $s_x^2 = 48$

A second inspector, B, measured the weight, y g, of each of a random sample of 15 oranges of variety Q with the following results:

   149   146   151   142   153   144   148   152
   140   152   137   140   153   155   158
   $\bar{y} = 148$ $s_y^2 = 39$

(a) Indicate a possible source of bias in the collection of these data and suggest how it could have been avoided. *(2 marks)*

It has been established that the weights of oranges are approximately normally distributed.

(b) Test, at the 5% significance level, the hypothesis that there is no difference in variability between the weights of the two varieties of oranges. *(6 marks)*

(c) Hence, stating null and alternative hypotheses, and using a 5% significance level, investigate the claim that the mean weight of oranges of variety P exceeds that of oranges of variety Q. *(11 marks)*

6 While collecting data on fitness levels the manager of a health club measured the pulse rate of those members present in the gymnasium after they had performed a predetermined number of step-ups. The table below shows the number of step-ups, x, and the pulse rates, y beats per minute.

Member	A	B	C	D	E	F	G	H
x	15	50	35	25	20	30	10	45
y	114	155	132	112	96	105	78	113

$S_{xx} = 1387.5$, $S_{yy} = 3704.875$, r $= 0.792\,252$

The regression equation is $y = 75.9 + 1.29x$.

(a) Illustrate the data using a scatter diagram. Draw the regression line on your scatter diagram. (*4 marks*)

(b) Assuming the model $Y = \alpha + \beta x + \varepsilon$, where ε is $N(0, \sigma^2)$:
   (i) estimate σ^2, (*3 marks*)
   (ii) investigate, using a 5% significance level, whether pulse rate increases with the number of step-ups. (*6 marks*)

(c) Comment on the suitability of the model you have been told to assume. (*3 marks*)

Appendix

Table 1 Cumulative binomial distribution function

The tabulated value is $P(X \leqslant x)$, where X has a binomial distribution with parameters n and p.

	x	0.01	0.02	0.03	0.04	0.05	0.06	0.07	0.08	0.09	0.10	0.15	0.20	0.25	0.30	0.35	0.40	0.45	0.50	x
n = 2	0	0.9801	0.9604	0.9409	0.9216	0.9025	0.8836	0.8649	0.8464	0.8281	0.8100	0.7225	0.6400	0.5625	0.4900	0.4225	0.3600	0.3025	0.2500	0
	1	0.9999	0.9996	0.9991	0.9984	0.9975	0.9964	0.9951	0.9936	0.9919	0.9900	0.9775	0.9600	0.9375	0.9100	0.8775	0.8400	0.7975	0.7500	1
	2	1.0000	1.0000	1.0000	1.0000	1.0000	1.0000	1.0000	1.0000	1.0000	1.0000	1.0000	1.0000	1.0000	1.0000	1.0000	1.0000	1.0000	1.0000	2
n = 3	0	0.9703	0.9412	0.9127	0.8847	0.8574	0.8306	0.8044	0.7787	0.7536	0.7290	0.6141	0.5120	0.4219	0.3430	0.2746	0.2160	0.1664	0.1250	0
	1	0.9997	0.9988	0.9974	0.9953	0.9928	0.9896	0.9860	0.9818	0.9772	0.9720	0.9393	0.8960	0.8438	0.7840	0.7183	0.6480	0.5747	0.5000	1
	2	1.0000	1.0000	1.0000	0.9999	0.9999	0.9998	0.9997	0.9995	0.9993	0.9990	0.9966	0.9920	0.9844	0.9730	0.9571	0.9360	0.9089	0.8750	2
	3				1.0000	1.0000	1.0000	1.0000	1.0000	1.0000	1.0000	1.0000	1.0000	1.0000	1.0000	1.0000	1.0000	1.0000	1.0000	3
n = 4	0	0.9606	0.9224	0.8853	0.8493	0.8145	0.7807	0.7481	0.7164	0.6857	0.6561	0.5220	0.4096	0.3164	0.2401	0.1785	0.1296	0.0915	0.0625	0
	1	0.9994	0.9977	0.9948	0.9909	0.9860	0.9801	0.9733	0.9656	0.9570	0.9477	0.8905	0.8192	0.7383	0.6517	0.5630	0.4752	0.3910	0.3125	1
	2	1.0000	1.0000	0.9999	0.9998	0.9995	0.9992	0.9987	0.9981	0.9973	0.9963	0.9880	0.9728	0.9492	0.9163	0.8735	0.8208	0.7585	0.6875	2
	3			1.0000	1.0000	1.0000	1.0000	1.0000	1.0000	0.9999	0.9999	0.9995	0.9984	0.9961	0.9919	0.9850	0.9744	0.9590	0.9375	3
	4									1.0000	1.0000	1.0000	1.0000	1.0000	1.0000	1.0000	1.0000	1.0000	1.0000	4
n = 5	0	0.9510	0.9039	0.8587	0.8154	0.7738	0.7339	0.6957	0.6591	0.6240	0.5905	0.4437	0.3277	0.2373	0.1681	0.1160	0.0778	0.0503	0.0313	0
	1	0.9990	0.9962	0.9915	0.9852	0.9774	0.9681	0.9575	0.9456	0.9326	0.9185	0.8352	0.7373	0.6328	0.5282	0.4284	0.3370	0.2562	0.1875	1
	2	1.0000	0.9999	0.9997	0.9994	0.9988	0.9980	0.9969	0.9955	0.9937	0.9914	0.9734	0.9421	0.8965	0.8369	0.7648	0.6826	0.5931	0.5000	2
	3		1.0000	1.0000	1.0000	1.0000	0.9999	0.9999	0.9998	0.9997	0.9995	0.9978	0.9933	0.9844	0.9692	0.9460	0.9130	0.8688	0.8125	3
	4						1.0000	1.0000	1.0000	1.0000	1.0000	0.9999	0.9997	0.9990	0.9976	0.9947	0.9898	0.9815	0.9688	4
	5											1.0000	1.0000	1.0000	1.0000	1.0000	1.0000	1.0000	1.0000	5
n = 6	0	0.9415	0.8858	0.8330	0.7828	0.7351	0.6899	0.6470	0.6064	0.5679	0.5314	0.3771	0.2621	0.1780	0.1176	0.0754	0.0467	0.0277	0.0156	0
	1	0.9985	0.9943	0.9875	0.9784	0.9672	0.9541	0.9392	0.9227	0.9048	0.8857	0.7765	0.6554	0.5339	0.4202	0.3191	0.2333	0.1636	0.1094	1
	2	1.0000	0.9998	0.9995	0.9988	0.9978	0.9962	0.9942	0.9915	0.9882	0.9842	0.9527	0.9011	0.8306	0.7443	0.6471	0.5443	0.4415	0.3438	2
	3		1.0000	1.0000	1.0000	0.9999	0.9999	0.9997	0.9995	0.9992	0.9987	0.9941	0.9830	0.9624	0.9295	0.8826	0.8208	0.7447	0.6563	3
	4					1.0000	1.0000	1.0000	1.0000	1.0000	0.9999	0.9996	0.9984	0.9954	0.9891	0.9777	0.9590	0.9308	0.8906	4
	5										1.0000	1.0000	0.9999	0.9998	0.9993	0.9982	0.9959	0.9917	0.9844	5
	6												1.0000	1.0000	1.0000	1.0000	1.0000	1.0000	1.0000	6
n = 7	0	0.9321	0.8681	0.8080	0.7514	0.6983	0.6485	0.6017	0.5578	0.5168	0.4783	0.3206	0.2097	0.1335	0.0824	0.0490	0.0280	0.0152	0.0078	0
	1	0.9980	0.9921	0.9829	0.9706	0.9556	0.9382	0.9187	0.8974	0.8745	0.8503	0.7166	0.5767	0.4449	0.3294	0.2338	0.1586	0.1024	0.0625	1
	2	1.0000	0.9997	0.9991	0.9980	0.9962	0.9937	0.9903	0.9860	0.9807	0.9743	0.9262	0.8520	0.7564	0.6471	0.5323	0.4199	0.3164	0.2266	2
	3		1.0000	1.0000	0.9999	0.9998	0.9996	0.9993	0.9988	0.9982	0.9973	0.9879	0.9667	0.9294	0.8740	0.8002	0.7102	0.6083	0.5000	3
	4				1.0000	1.0000	1.0000	1.0000	0.9999	0.9999	0.9998	0.9988	0.9953	0.9871	0.9712	0.9444	0.9037	0.8471	0.7734	4
	5								1.0000	1.0000	1.0000	0.9999	0.9996	0.9987	0.9962	0.9910	0.9812	0.9643	0.9375	5
	6											1.0000	1.0000	0.9999	0.9998	0.9994	0.9984	0.9963	0.9922	6
	7													1.0000	1.0000	1.0000	1.0000	1.0000	1.0000	7
n = 8	0	0.9227	0.8508	0.7837	0.7214	0.6634	0.6096	0.5596	0.5132	0.4703	0.4305	0.2725	0.1678	0.1001	0.0576	0.0319	0.0168	0.0084	0.0039	0
	1	0.9972	0.9897	0.9777	0.9619	0.9428	0.9208	0.8965	0.8702	0.8423	0.8131	0.6572	0.5033	0.3671	0.2553	0.1691	0.1064	0.0632	0.0352	1
	2	0.9999	0.9996	0.9987	0.9969	0.9942	0.9904	0.9853	0.9789	0.9711	0.9619	0.8948	0.7969	0.6785	0.5518	0.4278	0.3154	0.2201	0.1445	2
	3	1.0000	1.0000	0.9999	0.9998	0.9996	0.9993	0.9987	0.9978	0.9966	0.9950	0.9786	0.9437	0.8862	0.8059	0.7064	0.5941	0.4770	0.3633	3
	4			1.0000	1.0000	1.0000	1.0000	0.9999	0.9999	0.9997	0.9996	0.9971	0.9896	0.9727	0.9420	0.8939	0.8263	0.7396	0.6367	4
	5							1.0000	1.0000	1.0000	1.0000	0.9998	0.9988	0.9958	0.9887	0.9747	0.9502	0.9115	0.8555	5
	6											1.0000	0.9999	0.9996	0.9987	0.9964	0.9915	0.9819	0.9648	6
	7												1.0000	1.0000	0.9999	0.9998	0.9993	0.9983	0.9961	7
	8														1.0000	1.0000	1.0000	1.0000	1.0000	8

Table 1 Cumulative binomial distribution function (cont.)

n = 9

x	0.01	0.02	0.03	0.04	0.05	0.06	0.07	0.08	0.09	0.10	0.15	0.20	0.25	0.30	0.35	0.40	0.45	0.50	x
0	0.9135	0.8337	0.7602	0.6925	0.6302	0.5730	0.5204	0.4722	0.4279	0.3874	0.2316	0.1342	0.0751	0.0404	0.0207	0.0101	0.0046	0.0020	0
1	0.9966	0.9869	0.9718	0.9522	0.9288	0.9022	0.8729	0.8417	0.8088	0.7748	0.5995	0.4362	0.3003	0.1960	0.1211	0.0705	0.0385	0.0195	1
2	0.9999	0.9994	0.9980	0.9955	0.9916	0.9862	0.9791	0.9702	0.9595	0.9470	0.8591	0.7382	0.6007	0.4628	0.3373	0.2318	0.1495	0.0898	2
3	1.0000	1.0000	0.9999	0.9997	0.9994	0.9987	0.9977	0.9963	0.9943	0.9917	0.9661	0.9144	0.8343	0.7297	0.6089	0.4826	0.3614	0.2539	3
4			1.0000	1.0000	1.0000	0.9999	0.9998	0.9997	0.9995	0.9991	0.9944	0.9804	0.9511	0.9012	0.8283	0.7334	0.6214	0.5000	4
5						1.0000	1.0000	1.0000	1.0000	0.9999	0.9994	0.9969	0.9900	0.9747	0.9464	0.9006	0.8342	0.7461	5
6										1.0000	1.0000	0.9997	0.9987	0.9957	0.9888	0.9750	0.9502	0.9102	6
7												1.0000	0.9999	0.9996	0.9986	0.9962	0.9909	0.9805	7
8													1.0000	1.0000	0.9999	0.9997	0.9992	0.9980	8
9															1.0000	1.0000	1.0000	1.0000	9

n = 10

x	0.01	0.02	0.03	0.04	0.05	0.06	0.07	0.08	0.09	0.10	0.15	0.20	0.25	0.30	0.35	0.40	0.45	0.50	x
0	0.9044	0.8171	0.7374	0.6648	0.5987	0.5386	0.4840	0.4344	0.3894	0.3487	0.1969	0.1074	0.0563	0.0282	0.0135	0.0060	0.0025	0.0010	0
1	0.9957	0.9838	0.9655	0.9418	0.9139	0.8824	0.8483	0.8121	0.7746	0.7361	0.5443	0.3758	0.2440	0.1493	0.0860	0.0464	0.0233	0.0107	1
2	0.9999	0.9991	0.9972	0.9938	0.9885	0.9812	0.9717	0.9599	0.9460	0.9298	0.8202	0.6778	0.5256	0.3828	0.2616	0.1673	0.0996	0.0547	2
3	1.0000	1.0000	0.9999	0.9996	0.9990	0.9980	0.9964	0.9942	0.9912	0.9872	0.9500	0.8791	0.7759	0.6496	0.5138	0.3823	0.2660	0.1719	3
4			1.0000	1.0000	0.9999	0.9998	0.9997	0.9994	0.9990	0.9984	0.9901	0.9672	0.9219	0.8497	0.7515	0.6331	0.5044	0.3770	4
5					1.0000	1.0000	1.0000	1.0000	0.9999	0.9999	0.9986	0.9936	0.9803	0.9527	0.9051	0.8338	0.7384	0.6230	5
6									1.0000	1.0000	0.9999	0.9991	0.9965	0.9894	0.9740	0.9452	0.8980	0.8281	6
7											1.0000	0.9999	0.9996	0.9984	0.9952	0.9877	0.9726	0.9453	7
8												1.0000	1.0000	0.9999	0.9995	0.9983	0.9955	0.9893	8
9														1.0000	1.0000	0.9999	0.9997	0.9990	9
10																1.0000	1.0000	1.0000	10

n = 11

x	0.01	0.02	0.03	0.04	0.05	0.06	0.07	0.08	0.09	0.10	0.15	0.20	0.25	0.30	0.35	0.40	0.45	0.50	x
0	0.8953	0.8007	0.7153	0.6382	0.5688	0.5063	0.4501	0.3996	0.3544	0.3138	0.1673	0.0859	0.0422	0.0198	0.0088	0.0036	0.0014	0.0005	0
1	0.9948	0.9805	0.9587	0.9308	0.8981	0.8618	0.8228	0.7819	0.7399	0.6974	0.4922	0.3221	0.1971	0.1130	0.0606	0.0302	0.0139	0.0059	1
2	0.9998	0.9988	0.9963	0.9917	0.9848	0.9752	0.9630	0.9481	0.9305	0.9104	0.7788	0.6174	0.4552	0.3127	0.2001	0.1189	0.0652	0.0327	2
3	1.0000	1.0000	0.9998	0.9993	0.9984	0.9970	0.9947	0.9915	0.9871	0.9815	0.9306	0.8389	0.7133	0.5696	0.4256	0.2963	0.1911	0.1133	3
4			1.0000	1.0000	0.9999	0.9997	0.9995	0.9990	0.9983	0.9972	0.9841	0.9496	0.8854	0.7897	0.6683	0.5328	0.3971	0.2744	4
5					1.0000	1.0000	1.0000	0.9999	0.9998	0.9997	0.9973	0.9883	0.9657	0.9218	0.8513	0.7535	0.6331	0.5000	5
6									1.0000	1.0000	0.9997	0.9980	0.9924	0.9784	0.9499	0.9006	0.8262	0.7256	6
7											1.0000	0.9998	0.9988	0.9957	0.9878	0.9707	0.9390	0.8867	7
8												1.0000	0.9999	0.9994	0.9980	0.9941	0.9852	0.9673	8
9													1.0000	1.0000	0.9998	0.9993	0.9978	0.9941	9
10															1.0000	1.0000	0.9998	0.9995	10
11																		1.0000	11

n = 12

x	0.01	0.02	0.03	0.04	0.05	0.06	0.07	0.08	0.09	0.10	0.15	0.20	0.25	0.30	0.35	0.40	0.45	0.50	x
0	0.8864	0.7847	0.6938	0.6127	0.5404	0.4759	0.4186	0.3677	0.3225	0.2824	0.1422	0.0687	0.0317	0.0138	0.0057	0.0022	0.0008	0.0002	0
1	0.9938	0.9769	0.9514	0.9191	0.8816	0.8405	0.7967	0.7513	0.7052	0.6590	0.4435	0.2749	0.1584	0.0850	0.0424	0.0196	0.0083	0.0032	1
2	0.9998	0.9985	0.9952	0.9893	0.9804	0.9684	0.9532	0.9348	0.9134	0.8891	0.7358	0.5583	0.3907	0.2528	0.1513	0.0834	0.0421	0.0193	2
3	1.0000	0.9999	0.9997	0.9990	0.9978	0.9957	0.9925	0.9880	0.9820	0.9744	0.9078	0.7946	0.6488	0.4925	0.3467	0.2253	0.1345	0.0730	3
4		1.0000	1.0000	0.9999	0.9998	0.9996	0.9991	0.9984	0.9973	0.9957	0.9761	0.9274	0.8424	0.7237	0.5833	0.4382	0.3044	0.1938	4
5						1.0000	1.0000	0.9999	0.9998	0.9995	0.9954	0.9806	0.9456	0.8822	0.7873	0.6652	0.5269	0.3872	5
6									1.0000	1.0000	0.9999	0.9993	0.9961	0.9857	0.9614	0.9154	0.8418	0.6128	6
7										1.0000	0.9999	0.9994	0.9972	0.9905	0.9745	0.9427	0.8883	0.8062	7
8											1.0000	0.9999	0.9996	0.9983	0.9944	0.9847	0.9644	0.9270	8
9												1.0000	1.0000	0.9998	0.9992	0.9972	0.9921	0.9807	9
10													1.0000	1.0000	0.9999	0.9997	0.9989	0.9968	10
11															1.0000	1.0000	0.9999	0.9998	11
12																	1.0000	1.0000	12

n = 13

x	0.01	0.02	0.03	0.04	0.05	0.06	0.07	0.08	0.09	0.10	0.15	0.20	0.25	0.30	0.35	0.40	0.45	0.50	x
0	0.8775	0.7690	0.6730	0.5882	0.5133	0.4474	0.3893	0.3383	0.2935	0.2542	0.1209	0.0550	0.0238	0.0097	0.0037	0.0013	0.0004	0.0001	0
1	0.9928	0.9730	0.9436	0.9068	0.8646	0.8186	0.7702	0.7206	0.6707	0.6213	0.3983	0.2336	0.1267	0.0637	0.0296	0.0126	0.0049	0.0017	1
2	0.9997	0.9980	0.9938	0.9865	0.9755	0.9608	0.9422	0.9201	0.8946	0.8661	0.6920	0.5017	0.3326	0.2025	0.1132	0.0579	0.0269	0.0112	2
3	1.0000	0.9999	0.9995	0.9986	0.9969	0.9940	0.9897	0.9837	0.9758	0.9658	0.8820	0.7473	0.5843	0.4206	0.2783	0.1686	0.0929	0.0461	3
4		1.0000	1.0000	0.9999	0.9997	0.9993	0.9987	0.9976	0.9959	0.9935	0.9658	0.9009	0.7940	0.6543	0.5005	0.3530	0.2279	0.1334	4
5				1.0000	1.0000	0.9999	0.9999	0.9997	0.9995	0.9991	0.9925	0.9700	0.9198	0.8346	0.7159	0.5744	0.4268	0.2905	5
6							1.0000	1.0000	0.9999	0.9999	0.9987	0.9930	0.9757	0.9376	0.8705	0.7712	0.6437	0.5000	6
7										1.0000	0.9998	0.9988	0.9944	0.9818	0.9538	0.9023	0.8212	0.7095	7
8											1.0000	0.9998	0.9990	0.9960	0.9874	0.9679	0.9302	0.8666	8
9												1.0000	0.9999	0.9993	0.9975	0.9922	0.9797	0.9539	9
10													1.0000	0.9999	0.9997	0.9987	0.9959	0.9888	10
11														1.0000	1.0000	0.9999	0.9995	0.9983	11
12																1.0000	1.0000	0.9999	12
13																		1.0000	13

Table 1 Cumulative binomial distribution function (cont.)

	p →	0.01	0.02	0.03	0.04	0.05	0.06	0.07	0.08	0.09	0.10	0.15	0.20	0.25	0.30	0.35	0.40	0.45	0.50	p	x
n = 14	0	0.8687	0.7536	0.6528	0.5647	0.4877	0.4205	0.3620	0.3112	0.2670	0.2288	0.1028	0.0440	0.0178	0.0068	0.0024	0.0008	0.0002	0.0001		0
	1	0.9916	0.9690	0.9355	0.8941	0.8470	0.7963	0.7436	0.6900	0.6368	0.5846	0.3567	0.1979	0.1010	0.0475	0.0205	0.0081	0.0029	0.0009		1
	2	0.9997	0.9975	0.9923	0.9833	0.9699	0.9522	0.9302	0.9042	0.8745	0.8416	0.6479	0.4481	0.2811	0.1608	0.0839	0.0398	0.0170	0.0065		2
	3	1.0000	0.9999	0.9994	0.9981	0.9958	0.9920	0.9864	0.9786	0.9685	0.9559	0.8535	0.6982	0.5213	0.3552	0.2205	0.1243	0.0632	0.0287		3
	4		1.0000	1.0000	0.9998	0.9996	0.9990	0.9980	0.9965	0.9941	0.9908	0.9533	0.8702	0.7415	0.5842	0.4227	0.2793	0.1672	0.0898		4
	5					1.0000	0.9999	0.9998	0.9996	0.9992	0.9985	0.9885	0.9561	0.8883	0.7805	0.6405	0.4859	0.3373	0.2120		5
	6						1.0000	1.0000	1.0000	0.9999	0.9998	0.9978	0.9884	0.9617	0.9067	0.8164	0.6925	0.5461	0.3953		6
	7									1.0000	1.0000	0.9997	0.9976	0.9897	0.9685	0.9247	0.8499	0.7414	0.6047		7
	8											1.0000	0.9996	0.9978	0.9917	0.9757	0.9417	0.8811	0.7880		8
	9												1.0000	0.9997	0.9983	0.9940	0.9825	0.9574	0.9102		9
	10													1.0000	0.9998	0.9989	0.9961	0.9886	0.9713		10
	11														1.0000	0.9999	0.9994	0.9978	0.9935		11
	12															1.0000	0.9999	0.9997	0.9991		12
	13																1.0000	1.0000	0.9999		13
	14																		1.0000		14
n = 15	0	0.8601	0.7386	0.6333	0.5421	0.4633	0.3953	0.3367	0.2863	0.2430	0.2059	0.0874	0.0352	0.0134	0.0047	0.0016	0.0005	0.0001	0.0000		0
	1	0.9904	0.9647	0.9270	0.8809	0.8290	0.7738	0.7168	0.6597	0.6035	0.5490	0.3186	0.1671	0.0802	0.0353	0.0142	0.0052	0.0017	0.0005		1
	2	0.9996	0.9970	0.9906	0.9797	0.9638	0.9429	0.9171	0.8870	0.8531	0.8159	0.6042	0.3980	0.2361	0.1268	0.0617	0.0271	0.0107	0.0037		2
	3	1.0000	0.9998	0.9992	0.9976	0.9945	0.9896	0.9825	0.9727	0.9601	0.9444	0.8227	0.6482	0.4613	0.2969	0.1727	0.0905	0.0424	0.0176		3
	4		1.0000	0.9999	0.9998	0.9994	0.9986	0.9972	0.9950	0.9918	0.9873	0.9383	0.8358	0.6865	0.5155	0.3519	0.2173	0.1204	0.0592		4
	5			1.0000	1.0000	0.9999	0.9999	0.9997	0.9993	0.9987	0.9978	0.9832	0.9389	0.8516	0.7216	0.5643	0.4032	0.2608	0.1509		5
	6					1.0000	1.0000	1.0000	0.9999	0.9998	0.9997	0.9964	0.9819	0.9434	0.8689	0.7548	0.6098	0.4522	0.3036		6
	7								1.0000	1.0000	1.0000	0.9994	0.9958	0.9827	0.9500	0.8868	0.7869	0.6535	0.5000		7
	8											0.9999	0.9992	0.9958	0.9848	0.9578	0.9050	0.8182	0.6964		8
	9											1.0000	0.9999	0.9992	0.9963	0.9876	0.9662	0.9231	0.8491		9
	10												1.0000	0.9999	0.9993	0.9972	0.9907	0.9745	0.9408		10
	11													1.0000	0.9999	0.9995	0.9981	0.9937	0.9824		11
	12														1.0000	0.9999	0.9997	0.9989	0.9963		12
	13															1.0000	1.0000	0.9999	0.9995		13
	14																	1.0000	1.0000		14
n = 20	0	0.8179	0.6676	0.5438	0.4420	0.3585	0.2901	0.2342	0.1887	0.1516	0.1216	0.0388	0.0115	0.0032	0.0008	0.0002	0.0000	0.0000	0.0000		0
	1	0.9831	0.9401	0.8802	0.8103	0.7358	0.6605	0.5869	0.5169	0.4516	0.3917	0.1756	0.0692	0.0243	0.0076	0.0021	0.0005	0.0001	0.0000		1
	2	0.9990	0.9929	0.9790	0.9561	0.9245	0.8850	0.8390	0.7879	0.7334	0.6769	0.4049	0.2061	0.0913	0.0355	0.0121	0.0036	0.0009	0.0002		2
	3	1.0000	0.9994	0.9973	0.9926	0.9841	0.9710	0.9529	0.9294	0.9007	0.8670	0.6477	0.4114	0.2252	0.1071	0.0444	0.0160	0.0049	0.0013		3
	4		1.0000	0.9997	0.9990	0.9974	0.9944	0.9893	0.9817	0.9710	0.9568	0.8298	0.6296	0.4148	0.2375	0.1182	0.0510	0.0189	0.0059		4
	5			1.0000	0.9999	0.9997	0.9991	0.9981	0.9962	0.9932	0.9887	0.9327	0.8042	0.6172	0.4164	0.2454	0.1256	0.0553	0.0207		5
	6				1.0000	1.0000	0.9999	0.9997	0.9994	0.9987	0.9976	0.9781	0.9133	0.7858	0.6080	0.4166	0.2500	0.1299	0.0577		6
	7						1.0000	1.0000	0.9999	0.9998	0.9996	0.9941	0.9679	0.8982	0.7723	0.6010	0.4159	0.2520	0.1316		7
	8								1.0000	1.0000	0.9999	0.9987	0.9900	0.9591	0.8867	0.7624	0.5956	0.4143	0.2517		8
	9										1.0000	0.9998	0.9974	0.9861	0.9520	0.8782	0.7553	0.5914	0.4119		9
	10											1.0000	0.9994	0.9961	0.9829	0.9468	0.8725	0.7507	0.5881		10
	11												0.9999	0.9991	0.9949	0.9804	0.9435	0.8692	0.7483		11
	12												1.0000	0.9998	0.9987	0.9940	0.9790	0.9420	0.8684		12
	13													1.0000	0.9997	0.9985	0.9935	0.9786	0.9423		13
	14														1.0000	0.9997	0.9984	0.9936	0.9793		14
	15															1.0000	0.9997	0.9985	0.9941		15
	16																1.0000	0.9997	0.9987		16
	17																	1.0000	0.9998		17
	18																		1.0000		18
n = 25	0	0.7778	0.6035	0.4670	0.3604	0.2774	0.2129	0.1630	0.1244	0.0946	0.0718	0.0172	0.0038	0.0008	0.0001	0.0000	0.0000	0.0000	0.0000		0
	1	0.9742	0.9114	0.8280	0.7358	0.6424	0.5527	0.4696	0.3947	0.3286	0.2712	0.0931	0.0274	0.0070	0.0016	0.0003	0.0001	0.0000	0.0000		1
	2	0.9980	0.9868	0.9620	0.9235	0.8729	0.8129	0.7466	0.6768	0.6063	0.5371	0.2537	0.0982	0.0321	0.0090	0.0021	0.0004	0.0001	0.0000		2
	3	0.9999	0.9986	0.9938	0.9835	0.9659	0.9402	0.9064	0.8649	0.8169	0.7636	0.4711	0.2340	0.0962	0.0332	0.0097	0.0024	0.0005	0.0001		3
	4	1.0000	0.9999	0.9992	0.9972	0.9928	0.9850	0.9726	0.9549	0.9314	0.9020	0.6821	0.4207	0.2137	0.0905	0.0320	0.0095	0.0023	0.0005		4
	5		1.0000	0.9999	0.9996	0.9988	0.9969	0.9935	0.9877	0.9790	0.9666	0.8385	0.6167	0.3783	0.1935	0.0826	0.0294	0.0086	0.0020		5
	6			1.0000	1.0000	0.9998	0.9995	0.9987	0.9972	0.9946	0.9905	0.9305	0.7800	0.5611	0.3407	0.1734	0.0736	0.0258	0.0073		6
	7					1.0000	1.0000	0.9998	0.9995	0.9989	0.9977	0.9745	0.8909	0.7265	0.5118	0.3061	0.1536	0.0639	0.0216		7
	8						1.0000	1.0000	0.9999	0.9998	0.9995	0.9920	0.9532	0.8506	0.6769	0.4668	0.2735	0.1340	0.0539		8
	9								1.0000	1.0000	0.9999	0.9979	0.9827	0.9287	0.8106	0.6303	0.4246	0.2424	0.1148		9
	10										1.0000	0.9995	0.9944	0.9703	0.9022	0.7712	0.5858	0.3843	0.2122		10
	11											0.9999	0.9985	0.9893	0.9558	0.8746	0.7323	0.5426	0.3450		11
	12											1.0000	0.9996	0.9966	0.9825	0.9396	0.8462	0.6937	0.5000		12
	13												0.9999	0.9991	0.9940	0.9745	0.9222	0.8173	0.6550		13
	14												1.0000	0.9998	0.9982	0.9907	0.9656	0.9040	0.7878		14
	15													1.0000	0.9995	0.9971	0.9868	0.9560	0.8852		15
	16														0.9999	0.9992	0.9957	0.9826	0.9461		16
	17														1.0000	0.9998	0.9988	0.9942	0.9784		17
	18															1.0000	0.9997	0.9984	0.9927		18
	19																0.9999	0.9996	0.9980		19
	20																1.0000	0.9999	0.9995		20
	21																	1.0000	0.9999		21
	22																		1.0000		22

Table 1 Cumulative binomial distribution function (cont.)

x	0.01	0.02	0.03	0.04	0.05	0.06	0.07	0.08	0.09	0.10	0.15	0.20	0.25	0.30	0.35	0.40	0.45	0.50	x
n = 30 0	0.7397	0.5455	0.4010	0.2939	0.2146	0.1563	0.1134	0.0820	0.0591	0.0424	0.0076	0.0012	0.0002	0.0000	0.0000	0.0000	0.0000	0.0000	0
1	0.9639	0.8795	0.7731	0.6612	0.5535	0.4555	0.3694	0.2958	0.2343	0.1837	0.0480	0.0105	0.0020	0.0003	0.0000	0.0000	0.0000	0.0000	1
2	0.9967	0.9783	0.9399	0.8831	0.8122	0.7324	0.6487	0.5654	0.4855	0.4114	0.1514	0.0442	0.0106	0.0021	0.0003	0.0000	0.0000	0.0000	2
3	0.9998	0.9971	0.9881	0.9694	0.9392	0.8974	0.8450	0.7842	0.7175	0.6474	0.3217	0.1227	0.0374	0.0093	0.0019	0.0003	0.0000	0.0000	3
4	1.0000	0.9997	0.9982	0.9937	0.9844	0.9685	0.9447	0.9126	0.8723	0.8245	0.5245	0.2552	0.0979	0.0302	0.0075	0.0015	0.0002	0.0000	4
5		1.0000	0.9998	0.9989	0.9967	0.9921	0.9838	0.9707	0.9519	0.9268	0.7106	0.4275	0.2026	0.0766	0.0233	0.0057	0.0011	0.0002	5
6			1.0000	0.9999	0.9994	0.9983	0.9960	0.9918	0.9848	0.9742	0.8474	0.6070	0.3481	0.1595	0.0586	0.0172	0.0040	0.0007	6
7				1.0000	0.9999	0.9997	0.9992	0.9980	0.9959	0.9922	0.9302	0.7608	0.5143	0.2814	0.1238	0.0435	0.0121	0.0026	7
8						1.0000	1.0000	0.9996	0.9990	0.9980	0.9722	0.8713	0.6736	0.4315	0.2247	0.0940	0.0312	0.0081	8
9							1.0000	0.9999	0.9998	0.9995	0.9903	0.9389	0.8034	0.5888	0.3575	0.1763	0.0694	0.0214	9
10								1.0000	1.0000	0.9999	0.9971	0.9744	0.8943	0.7304	0.5078	0.2915	0.1350	0.0494	10
11										1.0000	0.9992	0.9905	0.9493	0.8407	0.6548	0.4311	0.2327	0.1002	11
12											0.9998	0.9969	0.9784	0.9155	0.7802	0.5785	0.3592	0.1808	12
13											1.0000	0.9991	0.9918	0.9599	0.8737	0.7145	0.5025	0.2923	13
14												0.9998	0.9973	0.9831	0.9348	0.8246	0.6448	0.4278	14
15												0.9999	0.9992	0.9936	0.9699	0.9029	0.7691	0.5722	15
16												1.0000	0.9998	0.9979	0.9876	0.9519	0.8644	0.7077	16
17													0.9999	0.9994	0.9955	0.9788	0.9286	0.8192	17
18													1.0000	0.9998	0.9986	0.9917	0.9666	0.8998	18
19														1.0000	0.9996	0.9971	0.9862	0.9506	19
20															0.9999	0.9991	0.9950	0.9786	20
21															1.0000	0.9998	0.9984	0.9919	21
22																1.0000	0.9996	0.9974	22
23																	0.9999	0.9993	23
24																	1.0000	0.9998	24
25																		1.0000	25

x	0.01	0.02	0.03	0.04	0.05	0.06	0.07	0.08	0.09	0.10	0.15	0.20	0.25	0.30	0.35	0.40	0.45	0.50	x
n = 40 0	0.6690	0.4457	0.2957	0.1954	0.1285	0.0842	0.0549	0.0356	0.0230	0.0148	0.0015	0.0001	0.0000	0.0000	0.0000	0.0000	0.0000	0.0000	0
1	0.9393	0.8095	0.6615	0.5210	0.3991	0.2990	0.2201	0.1594	0.1140	0.0805	0.0212	0.0015	0.0001	0.0000	0.0000	0.0000	0.0000	0.0000	1
2	0.9925	0.9543	0.8822	0.7855	0.6767	0.5665	0.4625	0.3694	0.2894	0.2228	0.0486	0.0079	0.0010	0.0001	0.0000	0.0000	0.0000	0.0000	2
3	0.9993	0.9918	0.9686	0.9252	0.8619	0.7827	0.6937	0.6007	0.5092	0.4231	0.1302	0.0285	0.0047	0.0006	0.0001	0.0000	0.0000	0.0000	3
4	1.0000	0.9988	0.9933	0.9790	0.9520	0.9104	0.8546	0.7868	0.7103	0.6290	0.2633	0.0759	0.0160	0.0026	0.0003	0.0000	0.0000	0.0000	4
5		0.9999	0.9988	0.9951	0.9861	0.9691	0.9419	0.9033	0.8535	0.7937	0.4325	0.1613	0.0433	0.0086	0.0013	0.0001	0.0000	0.0000	5
6		1.0000	0.9998	0.9990	0.9966	0.9909	0.9801	0.9624	0.9361	0.9005	0.6077	0.2859	0.0962	0.0238	0.0044	0.0006	0.0001	0.0000	6
7			1.0000	0.9998	0.9993	0.9977	0.9942	0.9873	0.9758	0.9581	0.7559	0.4371	0.1820	0.0553	0.0124	0.0021	0.0002	0.0000	7
8				1.0000	0.9999	0.9995	0.9985	0.9963	0.9919	0.9845	0.8646	0.5931	0.2998	0.1110	0.0303	0.0061	0.0009	0.0001	8
9					1.0000	0.9999	0.9997	0.9990	0.9976	0.9949	0.9328	0.7318	0.4395	0.1959	0.0644	0.0156	0.0027	0.0003	9
10						1.0000	0.9999	0.9998	0.9994	0.9985	0.9701	0.8392	0.5839	0.3087	0.1215	0.0352	0.0074	0.0011	10
11							1.0000	1.0000	0.9999	0.9996	0.9880	0.9125	0.7151	0.4406	0.2053	0.0709	0.0179	0.0032	11
12								1.0000	1.0000	0.9999	0.9957	0.9568	0.8209	0.5772	0.3143	0.1285	0.0386	0.0083	12
13										1.0000	0.9986	0.9806	0.8968	0.7032	0.4408	0.2112	0.0751	0.0192	13
14											0.9996	0.9921	0.9456	0.8074	0.5721	0.3174	0.1326	0.0403	14
15											0.9999	0.9971	0.9738	0.8849	0.6946	0.4402	0.2142	0.0769	15
16											1.0000	0.9990	0.9884	0.9367	0.7978	0.5681	0.3185	0.1341	16
17												0.9997	0.9953	0.9680	0.8761	0.6885	0.4391	0.2148	17
18												0.9999	0.9983	0.9852	0.9301	0.7911	0.5651	0.3179	18
19												1.0000	0.9994	0.9937	0.9637	0.8702	0.6844	0.4373	19
20													0.9998	0.9976	0.9827	0.9256	0.7870	0.5627	20
21													1.0000	0.9991	0.9925	0.9608	0.8669	0.6821	21
22														0.9997	0.9970	0.9811	0.9233	0.7852	22
23														0.9999	0.9989	0.9917	0.9595	0.8659	23
24														1.0000	0.9996	0.9966	0.9804	0.9231	24
25															0.9999	0.9988	0.9914	0.9597	25
26															1.0000	0.9996	0.9966	0.9808	26
27																0.9999	0.9988	0.9917	27
28																1.0000	0.9996	0.9968	28
29																	0.9999	0.9989	29
30																	1.0000	0.9997	30
31																		0.9999	31
32																		1.0000	32

Table 1 Cumulative binomial distribution function (cont.)

x	0.01	0.02	0.03	0.04	0.05	0.06	0.07	0.08	0.09	0.10	0.15	0.20	0.25	0.30	0.35	0.40	0.45	0.50	x
$n = 50$ 0	0.6050	0.3642	0.2181	0.1299	0.0769	0.0453	0.0266	0.0155	0.0090	0.0052	0.0003	0.0000	0.0000	0.0000	0.0000	0.0000	0.0000	0.0000	0
1	0.9106	0.7358	0.5553	0.4005	0.2794	0.1900	0.1265	0.0827	0.0532	0.0338	0.0029	0.0002	0.0000	0.0000	0.0000	0.0000	0.0000	0.0000	1
2	0.9862	0.9216	0.8108	0.6767	0.5405	0.4162	0.3108	0.2260	0.1605	0.1117	0.0142	0.0013	0.0001	0.0000	0.0000	0.0000	0.0000	0.0000	2
3	0.9984	0.9822	0.9372	0.8609	0.7604	0.6473	0.5327	0.4253	0.3303	0.2503	0.0460	0.0057	0.0005	0.0000	0.0000	0.0000	0.0000	0.0000	3
4	0.9999	0.9968	0.9832	0.9510	0.8964	0.8206	0.7290	0.6290	0.5277	0.4312	0.1121	0.0185	0.0021	0.0002	0.0000	0.0000	0.0000	0.0000	4
5	1.0000	0.9995	0.9963	0.9856	0.9622	0.9224	0.8650	0.7919	0.7072	0.6161	0.2194	0.0480	0.0070	0.0007	0.0001	0.0000	0.0000	0.0000	5
6		0.9999	0.9993	0.9964	0.9882	0.9711	0.9417	0.8981	0.8404	0.7702	0.3613	0.1034	0.0194	0.0025	0.0002	0.0000	0.0000	0.0000	6
7		1.0000	0.9999	0.9992	0.9968	0.9906	0.9780	0.9562	0.9232	0.8779	0.5188	0.1904	0.0453	0.0073	0.0008	0.0001	0.0000	0.0000	7
8			1.0000	0.9999	0.9992	0.9973	0.9927	0.9833	0.9672	0.9421	0.6681	0.3073	0.0916	0.0183	0.0025	0.0002	0.0000	0.0000	8
9				1.0000	0.9998	0.9993	0.9978	0.9944	0.9875	0.9755	0.7911	0.4437	0.1637	0.0402	0.0067	0.0008	0.0001	0.0000	9
10					1.0000	0.9998	0.9994	0.9983	0.9957	0.9906	0.8801	0.5836	0.2622	0.0789	0.0160	0.0022	0.0002	0.0000	10
11						1.0000	0.9999	0.9995	0.9987	0.9968	0.9372	0.7107	0.3816	0.1390	0.0342	0.0057	0.0006	0.0000	11
12							1.0000	0.9999	0.9996	0.9990	0.9699	0.8139	0.5110	0.2229	0.0661	0.0133	0.0018	0.0002	12
13								1.0000	0.9999	0.9997	0.9868	0.8894	0.6370	0.3279	0.1163	0.0280	0.0045	0.0005	13
14									1.0000	0.9999	0.9947	0.9393	0.7481	0.4468	0.1878	0.0540	0.0104	0.0013	14
15										1.0000	0.9981	0.9692	0.8369	0.5692	0.2801	0.0955	0.0220	0.0033	15
16											0.9993	0.9856	0.9017	0.6839	0.3889	0.1561	0.0427	0.0077	16
17											0.9998	0.9937	0.9449	0.7822	0.5060	0.2369	0.0765	0.0164	17
18											0.9999	0.9975	0.9713	0.8594	0.6216	0.3356	0.1273	0.0325	18
19											1.0000	0.9991	0.9861	0.9152	0.7264	0.4465	0.1974	0.0595	19
20												0.9997	0.9937	0.9522	0.8139	0.5610	0.2862	0.1013	20
21												0.9999	0.9974	0.9749	0.8813	0.6701	0.3900	0.1611	21
22												1.0000	0.9990	0.9877	0.9290	0.7660	0.5019	0.2399	22
23													0.9996	0.9944	0.9604	0.8438	0.6134	0.3359	23
24													0.9999	0.9976	0.9793	0.9022	0.7160	0.4439	24
25													1.0000	0.9991	0.9900	0.9427	0.8034	0.5561	25
26														0.9997	0.9955	0.9686	0.8721	0.6641	26
27														0.9999	0.9981	0.9840	0.9220	0.7601	27
28														1.0000	0.9993	0.9924	0.9556	0.8389	28
29															0.9997	0.9966	0.9765	0.8987	29
30															0.9999	0.9986	0.9884	0.9405	30
31															1.0000	0.9995	0.9947	0.9675	31
32																0.9998	0.9978	0.9836	32
33																0.9999	0.9991	0.9923	33
34																1.0000	0.9997	0.9967	34
35																	0.9999	0.9987	35
36																	1.0000	0.9995	36
37																		0.9998	37
38																		1.0000	38

Table 2 Cumulative Poisson distribution function

The tabulated value is $P(X \leqslant x)$, where X has a Poisson distribution with mean λ.

x \ λ	0.1	0.2	0.3	0.4	0.5	0.6	0.7	0.8	0.9	1.0	1.2	1.4	1.6	1.6	λ \ x
0	0.9048	0.8187	0.7408	0.6703	0.6065	0.5488	0.4966	0.4493	0.4066	0.3679	0.3012	0.2466	0.2019	0.1653	0
1	0.9953	0.9825	0.9631	0.9384	0.9098	0.8781	0.8442	0.8088	0.7725	0.7358	0.6626	0.5918	0.5249	0.4628	1
2	0.9998	0.9989	0.9964	0.9921	0.9856	0.9769	0.9659	0.9526	0.9371	0.9197	0.8795	0.8335	0.7834	0.7306	2
3	1.0000	0.9999	0.9997	0.9992	0.9982	0.9966	0.9942	0.9909	0.9865	0.9810	0.9662	0.9463	0.9212	0.8913	3
4		1.0000	1.0000	0.9999	0.9998	0.9996	0.9992	0.9986	0.9977	0.9963	0.9923	0.9857	0.9763	0.9636	4
5				1.0000	1.0000	1.0000	0.9999	0.9998	0.9997	0.9994	0.9985	0.9968	0.9940	0.9896	5
6							1.0000	1.0000	1.0000	0.9999	0.9997	0.9994	0.9987	0.9974	6
7										1.0000	1.0000	0.9999	0.9997	0.9994	7
8												1.0000	1.0000	0.9999	8
9														1.0000	9

x \ λ	2.0	2.2	2.4	2.6	2.8	3.0	3.2	3.4	3.6	3.8	4.0	4.5	5.0	5.5	λ \ x
0	0.1353	0.1108	0.0907	0.0743	0.0608	0.0498	0.0408	0.0334	0.0273	0.0224	0.0183	0.0111	0.0067	0.0041	0
1	0.4060	0.3546	0.3084	0.2674	0.2311	0.1991	0.1712	0.1468	0.1257	0.1074	0.0916	0.0611	0.0404	0.0266	1
2	0.6767	0.6227	0.5697	0.5184	0.4695	0.4232	0.3799	0.3397	0.3027	0.2689	0.2381	0.1736	0.1247	0.0884	2
3	0.8571	0.8194	0.7787	0.7360	0.6919	0.6472	0.6025	0.5584	0.5152	0.4735	0.4335	0.3423	0.2650	0.2017	3
4	0.9473	0.9275	0.9041	0.8774	0.8477	0.8153	0.7806	0.7442	0.7064	0.6678	0.6288	0.5321	0.4405	0.3575	4
5	0.9834	0.9751	0.9643	0.9510	0.9349	0.9161	0.8946	0.8705	0.8441	0.8156	0.7851	0.7029	0.6160	0.5289	5
6	0.9955	0.9925	0.9884	0.9828	0.9756	0.9665	0.9554	0.9421	0.9267	0.9091	0.8893	0.8311	0.7622	0.6860	6
7	0.9989	0.9980	0.9967	0.9947	0.9919	0.9881	0.9832	0.9769	0.9692	0.9599	0.9489	0.9134	0.8666	0.8095	7
8	0.9998	0.9995	0.9991	0.9985	0.9976	0.9962	0.9943	0.9917	0.9883	0.9840	0.9786	0.9597	0.9319	0.8944	8
9	1.0000	0.9999	0.9998	0.9996	0.9993	0.9989	0.9982	0.9973	0.9960	0.9942	0.9919	0.9829	0.9682	0.9462	9
10		1.0000	1.0000	0.9999	0.9998	0.9997	0.9995	0.9992	0.9987	0.9981	0.9972	0.9933	0.9863	0.9747	10
11				1.0000	1.0000	0.9999	0.9999	0.9998	0.9996	0.9994	0.9991	0.9976	0.9945	0.9890	11
12						1.0000	1.0000	0.9999	0.9999	0.9998	0.9997	0.9992	0.9980	0.9955	12
13								1.0000	1.0000	1.0000	0.9999	0.9997	0.9993	0.9983	13
14											1.0000	0.9999	0.9998	0.9994	14
15												1.0000	0.9999	0.9998	15
16													1.0000	0.9999	16
17														1.0000	17

x \ λ	6.0	6.5	7.0	7.5	8.0	8.5	9.0	9.5	10.0	11.0	12.0	13.0	14.0	15.0	λ \ r
0	0.0025	0.0015	0.0009	0.0006	0.0003	0.0002	0.0001	0.0001	0.0000	0.0000	0.0000	0.0000	0.0000	0.0000	0
1	0.0174	0.0113	0.0073	0.0047	0.0030	0.0019	0.0012	0.0008	0.0005	0.0002	0.0001	0.0000	0.0000	0.0000	1
2	0.0620	0.0430	0.0296	0.0203	0.0138	0.0093	0.0062	0.0042	0.0028	0.0012	0.0005	0.0002	0.0001	0.0000	2
3	0.1512	0.1118	0.0818	0.0591	0.0424	0.0301	0.0212	0.0149	0.0103	0.0049	0.0023	0.0011	0.0005	0.0002	3
4	0.2851	0.2237	0.1730	0.1321	0.0996	0.0744	0.0550	0.0403	0.0293	0.0151	0.0076	0.0037	0.0018	0.0009	4
5	0.4457	0.3690	0.3007	0.2414	0.1912	0.1496	0.1157	0.0885	0.0671	0.0375	0.0203	0.0107	0.0055	0.0028	5
6	0.6063	0.5265	0.4497	0.3782	0.3134	0.2562	0.2068	0.1649	0.1301	0.0786	0.0458	0.0259	0.0142	0.0076	6
7	0.7440	0.6728	0.5987	0.5246	0.4530	0.3856	0.3239	0.2687	0.2202	0.1432	0.0895	0.0540	0.0316	0.0180	7
8	0.8472	0.7916	0.7291	0.6620	0.5925	0.5231	0.4557	0.3918	0.3328	0.2320	0.1550	0.0998	0.0621	0.0374	8
9	0.9161	0.8774	0.8305	0.7764	0.7166	0.6530	0.5874	0.5218	0.4579	0.3405	0.2424	0.1658	0.1094	0.0699	9
10	0.9574	0.9332	0.9015	0.8622	0.8159	0.7634	0.7060	0.6453	0.5830	0.4599	0.3472	0.2517	0.1757	0.1185	10
11	0.9799	0.9661	0.9467	0.9208	0.8881	0.8487	0.8030	0.7520	0.6968	0.5793	0.4616	0.3532	0.2600	0.1848	11
12	0.9912	0.9840	0.9730	0.9573	0.9362	0.9091	0.8758	0.8364	0.7916	0.6887	0.5760	0.4631	0.3585	0.2676	12
13	0.9964	0.9929	0.9872	0.9784	0.9658	0.9486	0.9261	0.8981	0.8645	0.7813	0.6815	0.5730	0.4644	0.3632	13
14	0.9986	0.9970	0.9943	0.9897	0.9827	0.9726	0.9585	0.9400	0.9165	0.8540	0.7720	0.6751	0.5704	0.4657	14
15	0.9995	0.9988	0.9976	0.9954	0.9918	0.9862	0.9780	0.9665	0.9513	0.9074	0.8444	0.7636	0.6694	0.5681	15
16	0.9998	0.9996	0.9990	0.9980	0.9963	0.9934	0.9889	0.9823	0.9730	0.9441	0.8987	0.8355	0.7559	0.6641	16
17	0.9999	0.9998	0.9996	0.9992	0.9984	0.9970	0.9947	0.9911	0.9857	0.9678	0.9370	0.8905	0.8272	0.7489	17
18	1.0000	0.9999	0.9999	0.9997	0.9993	0.9987	0.9976	0.9957	0.9928	0.9823	0.9626	0.9302	0.8826	0.8195	18
19		1.0000	1.0000	0.9999	0.9997	0.9995	0.9989	0.9980	0.9965	0.9907	0.9787	0.9573	0.9235	0.8752	19
20				1.0000	0.9999	0.9998	0.9996	0.9991	0.9984	0.9953	0.9884	0.9750	0.9521	0.9170	20
21					1.0000	0.9999	0.9998	0.9996	0.9993	0.9977	0.9939	0.9859	0.9712	0.9469	21
22						1.0000	0.9999	0.9999	0.9997	0.9990	0.9970	0.9924	0.9833	0.9673	22
23							1.0000	0.9999	0.9999	0.9995	0.9985	0.9960	0.9907	0.9805	23
24								1.0000	1.0000	0.9998	0.9993	0.9980	0.9950	0.9888	24
25										0.9999	0.9997	0.9990	0.9974	0.9938	25
26										0.9999	0.9999	0.9995	0.9987	0.9967	26
27										1.0000	0.9999	0.9998	0.9994	0.9983	27
28											1.0000	0.9999	0.9997	0.9991	28
29												1.0000	0.9999	0.9996	29
30													0.9999	0.9998	30
31													1.0000	0.9999	31
32														1.0000	32

Table 3 Normal distribution function

The table gives the probability p that a normally distributed random variable Z, with mean $= 0$ and variance $= 1$, is less than or equal to z.

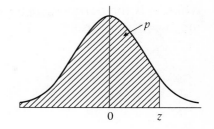

z	0.00	0.01	0.02	0.03	0.04	0.05	0.06	0.07	0.08	0.09	z
0.0	0.50000	0.50399	0.50798	0.51197	0.51595	0.51994	0.52392	0.52790	0.53188	0.53586	0.0
0.1	0.53983	0.54380	0.54776	0.55172	0.55567	0.55962	0.56356	0.56749	0.57142	0.57535	0.1
0.2	0.57926	0.58317	0.58706	0.59095	0.59483	0.59871	0.60257	0.60642	0.61026	0.61409	0.2
0.3	0.61791	0.62172	0.62552	0.62930	0.63307	0.63683	0.64058	0.64431	0.64803	0.65173	0.3
0.4	0.65542	0.65910	0.66276	0.66640	0.67003	0.67364	0.67724	0.68082	0.68439	0.68793	0.4
0.5	0.69146	0.69497	0.69847	0.70194	0.70540	0.70884	0.71226	0.71566	0.71904	0.72240	0.5
0.6	0.72575	0.72907	0.73237	0.73565	0.73891	0.74215	0.74537	0.74857	0.75175	0.75490	0.6
0.7	0.75804	0.76115	0.76424	0.76730	0.77035	0.77337	0.77637	0.77935	0.78230	0.78524	0.7
0.8	0.78814	0.79103	0.79389	0.79673	0.79955	0.80234	0.80511	0.80785	0.81057	0.81327	0.8
0.9	0.81594	0.81859	0.82121	0.82381	0.82639	0.82894	0.83147	0.83398	0.83646	0.83891	0.9
1.0	0.84134	0.84375	0.84614	0.84849	0.85083	0.85314	0.85543	0.85769	0.85993	0.86214	1.0
1.1	0.86433	0.86650	0.86864	0.87076	0.87286	0.87493	0.87698	0.87900	0.88100	0.88298	1.1
1.2	0.88493	0.88686	0.88877	0.89065	0.89251	0.89435	0.89617	0.89796	0.89973	0.90147	1.2
1.3	0.90320	0.90490	0.90658	0.90824	0.90988	0.91149	0.91309	0.91466	0.91621	0.91774	1.3
1.4	0.91924	0.92073	0.92220	0.92364	0.92507	0.92647	0.92785	0.92922	0.93056	0.93189	1.4
1.5	0.93319	0.93448	0.93574	0.93699	0.93822	0.93943	0.94062	0.94179	0.94295	0.94408	1.5
1.6	0.94520	0.94630	0.94738	0.94845	0.94950	0.05053	0.95154	0.95254	0.95352	0.95449	1.6
1.7	0.95543	0.95637	0.95728	0.95818	0.95907	0.95994	0.96080	0.96164	0.96246	0.96327	1.7
1.8	0.96407	0.96485	0.96562	0.96638	0.96712	0.96784	0.96856	0.96926	0.96995	0.97062	1.8
1.9	0.97128	0.97193	0.97257	0.97320	0.93781	0.97441	0.97500	0.97558	0.97615	0.97670	1.9
2.0	0.97725	0.97778	0.97831	0.97882	0.97932	0.97982	0.98030	0.98077	0.98124	0.98169	2.0
2.1	0.98214	0.98257	0.98300	0.98341	0.98382	0.98422	0.98461	0.98500	0.98537	0.98574	2.1
2.2	0.98610	0.98645	0.98679	0.98713	0.98745	0.98778	0.98809	0.98840	0.98870	0.98899	2.2
2.3	0.98928	0.98956	0.98983	0.99010	0.99036	0.99061	0.99086	0.99111	0.99134	0.99158	2.3
2.4	0.99180	0.99202	0.99224	0.99245	0.99266	0.99286	0.99305	0.99324	0.99343	0.99361	2.4
2.5	0.99379	0.99396	0.99413	0.99430	0.99446	0.99461	0.99477	0.99492	0.99506	0.99520	2.5
2.6	0.99534	0.99547	0.99560	0.99573	0.99585	0.99598	0.99609	0.99621	0.99632	0.99643	2.6
2.7	0.99653	0.99664	0.99674	0.99683	0.99693	0.99702	0.99711	0.99720	0.99728	0.99736	2.7
2.8	0.99744	0.99752	0.99760	0.99767	0.99774	0.99781	0.99788	0.99795	0.99801	0.99807	2.8
2.9	0.99813	0.99819	0.99825	0.99831	0.99836	0.99841	0.99846	0.99851	0.99856	0.99861	2.9
3.0	0.99865	0.99869	0.99874	0.99878	0.99882	0.99886	0.99889	0.99893	0.99896	0.99900	3.0
3.1	0.99903	0.99906	0.99910	0.99913	0.99916	0.99918	0.99921	0.99924	0.99926	0.99929	3.1
3.2	0.99931	0.99934	0.99936	0.99938	0.99940	0.99942	0.99944	0.99946	0.99948	0.99950	3.2
3.3	0.99952	0.99953	0.99955	0.99957	0.99958	0.99960	0.99961	0.99962	0.99964	0.99965	3.3
3.4	0.99966	0.99968	0.99969	0.99970	0.99971	0.99972	0.99973	0.99974	0.99975	0.99976	3.4
3.5	0.99977	0.99978	0.99978	0.99979	0.99980	0.99981	0.99981	0.99982	0.99983	0.99983	3.5
3.6	0.99984	0.99985	0.99985	0.99986	0.99986	0.99987	0.99987	0.99988	0.99988	0.99989	3.6
3.7	0.99989	0.99990	0.99990	0.99990	0.99991	0.99991	0.99992	0.99992	0.99992	0.99992	3.7
3.8	0.99993	0.99993	0.99993	0.99994	0.99994	0.99994	0.99994	0.99995	0.99995	0.99995	3.8
3.9	0.99995	0.99995	0.99996	0.99996	0.99996	0.99996	0.99996	0.99996	0.99997	0.99997	3.9

Table 4 Percentage points of the normal distribution

The table gives the values of z satisfying $P(Z \leqslant z) = p$, where Z is the normally distributed random variable with mean $= 0$ and variance $= 1$.

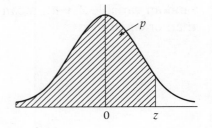

p	0.00	0.01	0.02	0.03	0.04	0.05	0.06	0.07	0.08	0.09	p
0.5	0.0000	0.0251	0.0502	0.0753	0.1004	0.1257	0.1510	0.1764	0.2019	0.2275	**0.5**
0.6	0.2533	0.2793	0.3055	0.3319	0.3585	0.3853	0.4125	0.4399	0.4677	0.4958	**0.6**
0.7	0.5244	0.5534	0.5828	0.6128	0.6433	0.6745	0.7063	0.7388	0.7722	0.8064	**0.7**
0.8	0.8416	0.8779	0.9154	0.9542	0.9945	1.0364	1.0803	1.1264	1.1750	1.2265	**0.8**
0.9	1.2816	1.3408	1.4051	1.4758	1.5548	1.6449	1.7507	1.8808	2.0537	2.3263	**0.9**

p	0.000	0.001	0.002	0.003	0.004	0.005	0.006	0.007	0.008	0.009	p
0.95	1.6449	1.6546	1.6646	1.6747	1.6849	1.6954	1.7060	1.7169	1.7279	1.7392	**0.95**
0.96	1.7507	1.7624	1.7744	1.7866	1.7991	1.8119	1.8250	1.8384	1.8522	1.8663	**0.96**
0.97	1.8808	1.8957	1.9110	1.9268	1.9431	1.9600	1.9774	1.9954	2.0141	2.0335	**0.97**
0.98	2.0537	2.0749	2.0969	2.1201	2.1444	2.1701	2.1973	2.2262	2.2571	2.2904	**0.98**
0.99	2.3263	2.3656	2.4089	2.4573	2.5121	2.5758	2.6521	2.7478	2.8782	3.0902	**0.99**

Table 5 Percentage points of the student's *t*-distribution

The table gives the values of *x* satisfying $P(X \leqslant x) = p$,
where *X* is a random variable having the student's *t*-distribution
with *v*-degrees of freedom.

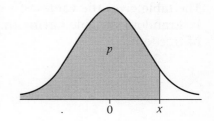

p	0.9	0.95	0.975	0.99	0.995
v					
1	3.078	6.314	12.706	31.821	63.657
2	1.886	2.920	4.303	6.965	9.925
3	1.638	2.353	3.182	4.541	5.841
4	1.533	2.132	2.776	3.747	4.604
5	1.476	2.015	2.571	3.365	4.032
6	1.440	1.943	2.447	3.143	3.707
7	1.415	1.895	2.365	2.998	3.499
8	1.397	1.860	2.306	2.896	3.355
9	1.383	1.833	2.262	2.821	3.250
10	1.372	1.812	2.228	2.764	3.169
11	1.363	1.796	2.201	2.718	3.106
12	1.356	1.782	2.179	2.681	3.055
13	1.350	1.771	2.160	2.650	3.012
14	1.345	1.761	2.145	2.624	2.977
15	1.341	1.753	2.131	2.602	2.947
16	1.337	1.746	2.121	2.583	2.921
17	1.333	1.740	2.110	2.567	2.898
18	1.330	1.734	2.101	2.552	2.878
19	1.328	1.729	2.093	2.539	2.861
20	1.325	1.725	2.086	2.528	2.845
21	1.323	1.721	2.080	2.518	2.831
22	1.321	1.717	2.074	2.508	2.819
23	1.319	1.714	2.069	2.500	2.807
24	1.318	1.711	2.064	2.492	2.797
25	1.316	1.708	2.060	2.485	2.787
26	1.315	1.706	2.056	2.479	2.779
27	1.314	1.703	2.052	2.473	2.771
28	1.313	1.701	2.048	2.467	2.763

p	0.9	0.95	0.975	0.99	0.995
v					
29	1.311	1.699	2.045	2.462	2.756
30	1.310	1.697	2.042	2.457	2.750
31	1.309	1.696	2.040	2.453	2.744
32	1.309	1.694	2.037	2.449	2.738
33	1.308	1.692	2.035	2.445	2.733
34	1.307	1.691	2.032	2.441	2.728
35	1.306	1.690	2.030	2.438	2.724
36	1.306	1.688	2.028	2.434	2.719
37	1.305	1.687	2.026	2.431	2.715
38	1.304	1.686	2.024	2.429	2.712
39	1.304	1.685	2.023	2.426	2.708
40	1.303	1.684	2.021	2.423	2.704
45	1.301	1.679	2.014	2.412	2.690
50	1.299	1.676	2.009	2.403	2.678
55	1.297	1.673	2.004	2.396	2.668
60	1.296	1.671	2.000	2.390	2.660
65	1.295	1.669	1.997	2.385	2.654
70	1.294	1.667	1.994	2.381	2.648
75	1.293	1.665	1.992	2.377	2.643
80	1.292	1.664	1.990	2.374	2.639
85	1.292	1.663	1.998	2.371	2.635
90	1.291	1.662	1.987	2.368	2.632
95	1.291	1.661	1.985	2.366	2.629
100	1.290	1.660	1.984	2.365	2.626
125	1.288	1.657	1.979	2.357	2.616
150	1.287	1.655	1.976	2.351	2.609
200	1.286	1.653	1.972	2.345	2.601
∞	1.282	1.645	1.960	2.326	2.576

Table 6 Percentage points of the χ^2-distribution

The table gives the values of x satisfying $P(X \leqslant x) = p$, where X is a random variable having the χ^2-distribution with v-degrees of freedom.

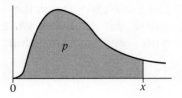

p	0.005	0.01	0.025	0.05	0.1	0.9	0.95	0.975	0.99	0.995	p
v											v
1	0.00004	0.0002	0.001	0.004	0.016	2.706	3.841	5.024	6.635	7.879	1
2	0.010	0.020	0.051	0.103	0.211	4.605	5.991	7.378	9.210	10.597	2
3	0.072	0.115	0.216	0.352	0.584	6.251	7.815	9.348	11.345	12.838	3
4	0.207	0.297	0.484	0.711	1.064	7.779	9.488	11.143	13.277	14.860	4
5	0.412	0.554	0.831	1.145	1.610	9.236	11.070	12.833	15.086	16.750	5
6	0.676	0.872	1.237	1.635	2.204	10.645	12.592	14.449	16.812	18.548	6
7	0.989	1.239	1.690	2.167	2.833	12.017	14.067	16.013	18.475	20.278	7
8	1.344	1.646	2.180	2.733	3.490	13.362	15.507	17.535	20.090	21.955	8
9	1.735	2.088	2.700	3.325	4.168	14.684	16.919	19.023	21.666	23.589	9
10	2.156	2.558	3.247	3.940	4.865	15.987	18.307	20.483	23.209	25.188	10
11	2.603	3.053	3.816	4.575	5.578	17.275	19.675	21.920	24.725	26.757	11
12	3.074	3.571	4.404	5.226	6.304	18.549	21.026	23.337	26.217	28.300	12
13	3.565	4.107	5.009	5.892	7.042	19.812	22.362	24.736	27.688	29.819	13
14	4.075	4.660	5.629	6.571	7.790	21.064	23.685	26.119	29.141	31.319	14
15	4.601	5.229	6.262	7.261	8.547	22.307	24.996	27.488	30.578	32.801	15
16	5.142	5.812	6.908	7.962	9.312	23.542	26.296	28.845	32.000	34.267	16
17	5.697	6.408	7.564	8.672	10.085	24.769	27.587	30.191	33.409	35.718	17
18	6.265	7.015	8.231	9.390	10.865	25.989	28.869	31.526	34.805	37.156	18
19	6.844	7.633	8.907	10.117	11.651	27.204	30.144	32.852	36.191	38.582	19
20	7.434	8.260	9.591	10.851	12.443	28.412	31.410	34.170	37.566	39.997	20
21	8.034	8.897	10.283	11.591	13.240	29.615	32.671	35.479	38.932	41.401	21
22	8.643	9.542	10.982	12.338	14.041	30.813	33.924	36.781	40.289	42.796	22
23	9.260	10.196	11.689	13.091	14.848	32.007	35.172	38.076	41.638	44.181	23
24	9.886	10.856	12.401	13.848	15.659	33.196	36.415	39.364	42.980	45.559	24
25	10.520	11.524	13.120	14.611	16.473	34.382	37.652	40.646	44.314	46.928	25
26	11.160	12.198	13.844	15.379	17.292	35.563	38.885	41.923	45.642	48.290	26
27	11.808	12.879	14.573	16.151	18.114	36.741	40.113	43.195	46.963	49.645	27
28	12.461	13.565	15.308	16.928	18.939	37.916	41.337	44.461	48.278	50.993	28
29	13.121	14.256	16.047	17.708	19.768	39.087	42.557	45.722	49.588	52.336	29
30	13.787	14.953	16.791	18.493	20.599	40.256	43.773	46.979	50.892	53.672	30
31	14.458	15.655	17.539	19.281	21.434	41.422	44.985	48.232	52.191	55.003	31
32	15.134	16.362	18.291	20.072	22.271	42.585	46.194	49.480	53.486	56.328	32
33	15.815	17.074	19.047	20.867	23.110	43.745	47.400	50.725	54.776	57.648	33
34	16.501	17.789	19.806	21.664	23.952	44.903	48.602	51.996	56.061	58.964	34
35	17.912	18.509	20.569	22.465	24.797	46.059	49.802	53.203	57.342	60.275	35
36	17.887	19.223	21.336	23.269	25.643	47.212	50.998	54.437	58.619	61.581	36
37	18.586	19.960	22.106	24.075	26.492	48.363	52.192	55.668	59.892	62.883	37
38	19.289	20.691	22.878	24.884	27.343	49.513	53.384	56.896	61.162	64.181	38
39	19.996	21.426	23.654	25.695	28.196	50.660	54.572	58.120	62.428	65.476	39
40	20.707	22.164	24.433	26.509	29.051	51.805	55.758	59.342	63.691	66.766	40
45	24.311	25.901	28.366	30.612	33.350	57.505	61.656	65.410	69.957	73.166	45
50	27.991	29.707	32.357	34.764	37.689	63.167	67.505	71.420	76.154	79.490	50
55	31.735	33.570	36.398	38.958	42.060	68.796	73.311	77.380	82.292	85.749	55
60	35.534	37.485	40.482	43.188	46.459	74.397	79.082	83.298	88.379	91.952	60
65	39.383	41.444	44.603	47.450	50.883	79.973	84.821	89.177	94.422	98.105	65
70	43.275	45.442	48.758	51.739	55.329	85.527	90.531	95.023	100.425	104.215	70
75	47.206	49.475	52.942	56.054	59.795	91.061	96.217	100.839	106.393	110.286	75
80	51.172	53.540	57.153	60.391	64.278	96.578	101.879	106.629	112.329	116.321	80
85	55.170	57.634	61.389	64.749	68.777	102.079	107.522	112.393	118.236	122.325	85
90	59.196	61.754	65.647	69.126	73.291	107.565	113.145	118.136	124.116	128.299	90
95	63.250	65.898	69.925	73.520	77.818	113.038	118.752	123.858	129.973	134.247	95
100	67.328	70.065	74.222	77.929	82.358	118.498	124.342	129.561	135.807	140.169	100

Table 7 Percentage points of the *F*-distribution

The tables give the values of x satisfying $P(X \leqslant x) = p$, where X is a random variable having the F-distribution with v_1 degrees of freedom in the numerator and v_2 degrees of freedom in the denominator.

F-distribution ($p = 0.995$)

Use for one-tail tests at significance level 0.5% or two-tail tests at significance level 1%.

v_1	1	2	3	4	5	6	7	8	9	10	11	12	15	20	25	30	40	50	100	∞	v_1
v_2																					v_2
1	16211	20000	21615	22500	23056	23437	23715	23925	24091	24224	24334	24426	24630	24836	24960	25044	25148	25211	25337	25464	1
2	198.5	199.0	199.2	199.2	199.3	199.3	199.4	199.4	199.4	199.4	199.4	199.4	199.4	199.4	199.5	199.5	199.5	199.5	199.5	199.5	2
3	55.55	49.80	47.47	46.19	45.39	44.84	44.43	44.13	43.88	43.69	43.52	43.39	43.08	42.78	42.59	42.47	42.31	42.21	42.02	41.83	3
4	31.33	26.28	24.26	23.15	22.46	21.97	21.62	21.35	21.14	20.97	20.82	20.70	20.44	20.17	20.00	19.89	19.75	19.67	19.50	19.32	4
5	22.78	18.31	16.53	16.56	14.94	14.51	14.20	13.96	13.77	13.62	13.49	13.38	13.15	12.90	12.76	12.66	12.53	12.45	12.30	12.14	5
6	18.635	14.544	12.917	12.028	11.464	11.073	10.786	10.566	10.391	10.250	10.133	10.034	9.814	9.589	9.451	9.358	9.241	9.170	9.026	8.879	6
7	16.236	12.404	10.882	10.050	9.522	9.155	8.885	8.678	8.514	8.380	8.270	8.176	7.968	7.754	7.623	7.534	7.422	7.354	7.217	7.076	7
8	14.688	11.042	9.596	8.805	8.302	7.952	7.694	7.496	7.339	7.211	7.104	7.015	6.814	6.608	6.482	6.396	6.288	6.222	6.088	5.951	8
9	13.614	10.107	8.717	7.956	7.471	7.134	6.885	6.693	6.541	6.417	6.314	6.227	6.032	5.832	5.708	5.625	5.519	5.454	5.322	5.188	9
10	12.826	9.427	8.081	7.343	6.827	6.545	6.302	6.116	5.968	5.847	5.746	5.661	5.471	5.274	5.153	5.071	4.966	4.902	4.772	4.639	10
11	12.226	8.912	7.600	6.881	6.442	6.102	5.865	5.682	5.537	5.418	5.320	5.236	5.049	4.855	4.736	4.654	4.551	4.488	4.359	4.226	11
12	11.754	8.510	7.226	6.521	6.071	5.757	5.525	5.345	5.202	5.085	4.988	4.906	4.721	4.530	4.412	4.331	4.228	4.165	4.037	3.904	12
13	11.374	8.186	6.926	6.233	5.791	5.482	5.253	5.076	4.935	4.820	4.724	4.643	4.460	4.270	4.153	4.073	3.970	3.908	3.780	3.647	13
14	11.060	7.922	6.680	5.998	5.562	5.257	5.031	4.857	4.717	4.603	4.508	4.428	4.247	4.059	3.942	3.862	3.760	3.697	3.569	3.436	14
15	10.798	7.701	6.476	5.803	5.372	5.071	4.847	4.674	4.536	4.424	4.329	4.250	4.070	3.883	3.766	3.687	3.585	3.523	3.394	3.260	15
20	9.944	6.986	5.818	5.174	4.762	4.472	4.257	4.090	3.956	3.847	3.756	3.678	3.502	3.318	3.203	3.123	3.022	2.959	2.828	2.690	20
25	9.475	6.598	5.462	4.835	4.433	4.150	3.939	3.776	3.645	3.537	3.447	3.370	3.196	3.013	2.898	2.819	2.716	2.652	2.519	2.377	25
30	9.180	6.355	5.239	4.623	4.228	3.949	3.742	3.580	3.450	3.344	3.255	3.179	3.006	2.823	2.708	2.628	2.524	2.459	2.232	2.176	30
40	8.828	6.066	4.976	4.374	3.986	3.713	3.509	3.350	3.222	3.117	3.028	2.953	2.781	2.598	2.482	2.401	2.296	2.230	2.088	1.932	40
50	8.626	5.902	4.826	4.232	3.849	3.579	3.376	3.219	3.092	2.988	2.900	2.825	2.653	2.470	2.353	2.272	2.164	2.097	1.951	1.786	50
100	8.241	5.589	4.542	3.963	3.589	3.325	3.127	2.972	2.847	2.744	2.657	2.583	2.411	2.227	2.108	2.024	1.912	1.840	1.681	1.485	100
∞	7.879	5.298	4.279	3.715	3.350	3.091	2.897	2.744	2.621	2.519	2.432	2.358	2.187	2.000	1.877	1.789	1.669	1.590	1.402	1.001	∞

F-distribution ($p = 0.99$)

Use for one-tail tests at significance level 1% or two-tail tests at significance level 2%.

v_1	1	2	3	4	5	6	7	8	9	10	11	12	15	20	25	30	40	50	100	∞	v_1
v_2																					v_2
1	4052	5000	5403	5625	5764	5859	5928	5981	6022	6056	6083	6106	6157	6209	6240	6261	6287	6303	6334	6366	1
2	98.50	99.00	99.17	99.25	99.30	99.33	99.36	99.37	99.39	99.40	99.41	99.42	99.43	99.45	99.46	99.47	99.47	99.48	99.49	99.50	2
3	34.12	30.82	29.46	28.71	28.24	27.91	27.67	27.49	27.35	27.23	27.13	27.05	26.87	26.69	26.58	26.50	26.41	26.35	26.24	26.13	3
4	21.20	18.00	16.69	15.98	15.52	15.21	14.98	14.80	14.66	14.55	14.45	14.37	14.20	14.02	13.91	13.84	13.75	13.69	13.58	13.46	4
5	16.26	13.27	12.06	11.39	10.97	10.67	10.46	10.29	10.16	10.05	9.96	9.89	9.72	9.55	9.45	9.38	9.29	9.24	9.13	9.02	5
6	13.745	10.925	9.780	9.148	8.746	8.466	8.260	8.102	7.976	7.874	7.790	7.718	7.559	7.396	7.296	7.229	7.143	7.091	6.987	6.880	6
7	12.246	9.574	8.451	7.847	7.460	7.191	6.993	6.840	6.719	6.620	6.538	6.469	6.314	6.155	6.058	5.992	5.908	5.858	5.755	5.650	7
8	11.259	8.649	7.591	7.006	6.632	6.371	6.178	6.029	5.911	5.814	5.734	5.667	5.515	5.359	5.263	5.198	5.116	5.065	4.963	4.859	8
9	10.561	8.022	6.992	6.422	6.057	5.802	5.613	5.467	5.351	5.257	5.178	5.111	4.962	4.808	4.713	4.649	4.567	4.517	4.415	4.311	9
10	10.044	7.559	6.552	5.994	5.636	5.386	5.200	5.057	4.942	4.849	4.772	4.706	4.558	4.405	4.311	4.247	4.165	4.115	4.014	3.909	10
11	9.646	7.206	6.217	5.668	5.316	5.069	4.886	4.744	4.632	4.539	4.462	4.397	4.251	4.099	4.005	3.941	3.860	3.810	3.708	3.602	11
12	9.330	6.927	5.953	5.412	5.064	4.821	4.640	4.499	4.388	4.296	4.220	4.155	4.010	3.858	3.765	3.701	3.619	3.569	3.467	3.361	12
13	9.047	6.701	5.739	5.205	4.862	4.620	4.441	4.302	4.191	4.100	4.025	3.960	3.815	3.665	3.571	3.507	3.425	3.375	3.272	3.165	13
14	8.862	6.515	5.564	5.035	4.695	4.465	4.278	4.140	4.030	3.939	3.864	3.800	3.656	3.505	3.412	3.348	3.266	3.215	3.112	3.004	14
15	8.683	6.359	5.417	4.893	4.556	4.318	4.142	4.004	3.895	3.805	3.730	3.666	3.522	3.372	3.278	3.214	3.132	3.081	2.977	2.868	15
20	8.096	5.849	4.938	4.431	4.103	3.871	3.699	3.564	3.457	3.368	3.294	3.231	3.088	2.938	2.843	2.778	2.695	2.643	2.535	2.421	20
25	7.770	5.568	4.675	4.177	3.855	3.627	3.457	3.324	3.217	3.129	3.056	2.993	2.850	2.699	2.604	2.538	2.453	2.400	2.289	2.169	25
30	7.562	5.390	4.510	4.018	3.699	3.473	3.304	3.173	3.067	2.979	2.906	2.843	2.700	2.549	2.453	2.386	2.299	2.245	2.131	2.006	30
40	7.314	5.179	4.313	3.828	3.514	3.291	3.124	2.993	2.888	2.801	2.727	2.665	2.522	2.369	2.271	2.203	2.114	2.058	1.938	1.805	40
50	7.171	5.057	4.199	3.720	3.408	3.186	3.020	2.890	2.785	2.698	2.625	2.562	2.419	2.265	2.167	2.098	2.007	1.949	1.825	1.683	50
100	6.895	4.824	3.984	3.513	3.206	2.988	2.823	2.694	2.590	2.503	2.430	2.368	2.223	2.067	1.965	1.893	1.797	1.735	1.598	1.427	100
∞	6.635	4.605	3.782	3.319	3.017	2.802	2.639	2.511	2.407	2.321	2.248	2.185	2.039	1.878	1.773	1.696	1.592	1.523	1.358	1.000	∞

Table 7 Percentage points of the *F*-distribution (continued)

F-distribution ($p = 0.975$)
Use for one-tail tests at significance level 2.5% or two-tail tests at significance level 5%.

v_1	1	2	3	4	5	6	7	8	9	10	11	12	15	20	25	30	40	50	100	∞	v_1
v_2																					v_2
1	647.8	799.5	864.2	899.6	921.8	937.1	948.2	956.7	963.3	968.6	973.0	976.7	984.9	993.1	998.1	1001.4	1005.6	1008.1	1013.2	1018.3	1
2	38.51	39.00	39.17	39.25	39.30	39.33	39.36	39.37	39.39	39.40	39.41	39.41	39.43	39.45	39.46	39.46	39.47	39.48	39.49	39.50	2
3	17.44	16.04	15.44	15.10	14.88	14.73	14.62	14.54	14.47	14.42	14.37	14.34	14.25	14.17	14.12	14.08	14.04	14.01	13.96	13.90	3
4	12.22	10.65	9.98	9.60	9.36	9.20	9.07	8.98	8.90	8.84	8.79	8.75	8.66	8.56	8.50	8.46	8.41	8.38	8.32	8.26	4
5	10.01	8.43	7.76	7.39	7.15	6.98	6.85	6.76	6.68	6.62	6.57	6.52	6.43	6.33	6.27	6.23	6.18	6.14	6.08	6.02	5
6	8.813	7.260	6.599	6.227	5.988	5.820	5.695	5.600	5.523	5.461	5.410	5.366	5.269	5.168	5.107	5.065	5.012	4.980	4.915	4.849	6
7	8.073	6.542	5.890	5.523	5.285	5.119	4.995	4.899	4.823	4.761	4.709	4.666	4.568	4.467	4.405	4.362	4.309	4.276	4.210	4.142	7
8	7.571	6.059	5.416	5.053	4.817	4.652	4.529	4.433	4.357	4.295	4.243	4.200	4.101	3.999	3.937	3.894	3.840	3.807	3.739	3.670	8
9	7.209	5.715	5.078	4.718	4.484	4.320	4.197	4.102	4.026	3.964	3.912	3.868	3.769	3.667	3.604	3.560	3.505	3.472	3.403	3.333	9
10	6.937	5.456	4.826	4.468	4.236	4.072	3.950	3.855	3.779	3.717	3.665	3.621	3.522	3.419	3.355	3.311	3.255	3.221	3.152	3.080	10
11	6.724	5.256	4.630	4.275	4.044	3.881	3.759	3.664	3.588	3.526	3.474	3.430	3.300	3.226	3.162	3.118	3.061	3.027	2.956	2.883	11
12	6.554	5.096	4.474	4.121	3.891	3.728	3.607	3.512	3.436	3.374	3.321	3.277	3.177	3.073	3.008	2.963	2.906	2.871	2.800	2.725	12
13	6.414	4.965	4.347	3.996	3.767	3.604	3.483	3.388	3.312	3.250	3.197	3.153	3.053	2.948	2.882	2.837	2.780	2.744	2.671	2.595	13
14	6.298	4.857	4.242	3.892	3.663	3.501	3.380	3.285	3.209	3.147	3.095	3.050	2.949	2.844	2.778	2.732	2.674	2.638	2.565	2.487	14
15	6.200	4.765	4.153	3.804	3.576	3.415	3.293	3.199	3.123	3.060	3.008	2.963	2.862	2.756	2.689	2.644	2.585	2.549	2.474	2.395	15
20	5.871	4.461	3.859	3.515	3.289	3.128	3.007	2.913	2.837	2.774	2.721	2.676	2.573	2.464	2.396	2.349	2.287	2.249	2.170	2.085	20
25	5.686	4.291	3.694	3.353	3.129	2.969	2.848	2.753	2.677	2.613	2.560	2.515	2.411	2.300	2.230	2.182	2.118	2.079	1.996	1.906	25
30	5.568	4.182	3.589	3.250	3.026	2.867	2.746	2.651	2.575	2.511	2.458	2.412	2.307	2.195	2.124	2.074	2.009	1.968	1.882	1.787	30
40	5.424	4.051	3.463	3.126	2.904	2.744	2.624	2.529	2.452	2.388	2.334	2.288	2.182	2.068	1.994	1.943	1.875	1.832	1.741	1.637	40
50	5.340	3.975	3.390	3.054	2.833	2.674	2.553	2.458	2.381	2.317	2.263	2.216	2.109	1.993	1.919	1.866	1.796	1.752	1.656	1.545	50
100	5.179	3.828	3.250	2.917	2.696	2.537	2.417	2.321	2.244	2.179	2.125	2.077	1.968	1.849	1.770	1.715	1.640	1.592	1.483	1.347	100
∞	5.024	3.689	3.116	2.786	2.567	2.408	2.288	2.192	2.114	2.048	1.993	1.945	1.833	1.708	1.626	1.566	1.484	1.428	1.296	1.000	∞

F-distribution ($p = 0.95$)
Use for one-tail tests at significance level 5% or two-tail tests at significance level 10%.

v_1	1	2	3	4	5	6	7	8	9	10	11	12	15	20	25	30	40	50	100	∞	v_1
v_2																					v_2
1	161.4	199.5	215.7	224.6	230.2	234.0	236.8	238.9	240.5	241.9	243.0	243.9	245.9	248.0	249.3	250.1	251.1	251.8	253.0	254.3	1
2	18.51	19.00	19.16	19.25	19.30	19.33	19.35	19.37	19.38	19.40	19.40	19.41	19.43	19.45	19.46	19.46	19.47	19.48	19.49	19.50	2
3	10.13	9.55	9.28	9.12	9.01	8.94	8.89	8.85	8.81	8.79	8.76	8.74	8.70	8.66	8.63	8.62	8.59	8.58	8.55	8.53	3
4	7.71	6.94	6.59	6.39	6.26	6.16	6.09	6.04	6.00	5.96	5.94	5.91	5.86	5.80	5.77	5.75	5.72	5.70	5.66	5.63	4
5	6.61	5.79	5.41	5.19	5.05	4.95	4.88	4.82	4.77	4.74	4.70	4.68	4.62	4.56	4.52	4.50	4.46	4.44	4.41	4.36	5
6	5.987	5.143	4.757	4.534	4.387	4.284	4.207	4.147	4.099	4.060	4.027	4.000	3.938	3.874	3.835	3.808	3.774	3.754	3.712	3.669	6
7	5.591	4.737	4.347	4.120	3.972	3.866	3.787	3.726	3.677	3.637	3.603	3.575	3.511	3.445	3.404	3.376	3.340	3.319	3.275	3.230	7
8	5.318	4.459	4.066	3.838	3.688	3.581	3.500	3.438	3.388	3.347	3.313	3.284	3.218	3.150	3.108	3.079	3.043	3.020	2.975	2.928	8
9	5.117	4.256	3.863	3.633	3.482	3.374	3.293	3.230	3.179	3.137	3.102	3.073	3.006	2.936	2.893	2.864	2.826	2.803	2.756	2.707	9
10	4.965	4.103	3.708	3.478	3.326	3.217	3.135	3.072	3.020	2.978	2.943	2.913	2.845	2.774	2.730	2.700	2.661	2.637	2.588	2.538	10
11	4.844	3.982	3.587	3.357	3.204	3.095	3.012	2.948	2.896	2.854	2.818	2.788	2.719	2.646	2.601	2.570	2.531	2.507	2.457	2.404	11
12	4.747	3.885	3.490	3.259	3.106	2.996	2.913	2.849	2.796	2.753	2.717	2.687	2.617	2.544	2.498	2.466	2.426	2.401	2.350	2.296	12
13	4.667	3.806	3.411	3.179	3.025	2.915	2.832	2.767	2.714	2.671	2.635	2.604	2.533	2.459	2.412	2.380	2.339	2.314	2.261	2.206	13
14	4.600	3.739	3.344	3.112	2.958	2.848	2.764	2.699	2.646	2.602	2.565	2.534	2.463	2.388	2.341	2.308	2.266	2.241	2.187	2.131	14
15	4.543	3.682	3.287	3.056	2.901	2.790	2.707	2.641	2.588	2.544	2.507	2.475	2.403	2.328	2.280	2.247	2.204	2.178	2.123	2.066	15
20	4.351	3.493	3.098	2.866	2.711	2.599	2.514	2.447	2.393	2.348	2.310	2.278	2.203	2.124	2.074	2.039	1.994	1.966	1.907	1.843	20
25	4.242	3.385	2.991	2.759	2.603	2.490	2.405	2.337	2.282	2.236	2.198	2.165	2.089	2.007	1.955	1.919	1.872	1.842	1.779	1.711	25
30	4.171	3.316	2.922	2.690	2.534	2.421	2.334	2.266	2.211	2.165	2.126	2.092	2.015	1.932	1.878	1.841	1.792	1.761	1.695	1.622	30
40	4.085	3.232	2.839	2.606	2.449	2.336	2.249	2.180	2.124	2.077	2.038	2.003	1.924	1.839	1.783	1.744	1.693	1.660	1.589	1.509	40
50	4.034	3.183	2.790	2.557	2.400	2.286	2.199	2.130	2.073	2.026	1.986	1.952	1.871	1.784	1.727	1.687	1.634	1.559	1.525	1.438	50
100	3.936	3.087	2.696	2.463	2.305	2.191	2.103	2.032	1.975	1.927	1.886	1.850	1.768	1.676	1.616	1.573	1.515	1.477	1.392	1.283	100
∞	3.841	2.996	2.605	2.372	2.214	2.099	2.010	1.938	1.880	1.831	1.789	1.752	1.666	1.571	1.506	1.459	1.394	1.350	1.243	1.000	∞

Answers

1 Linear combinations of independent normal variables

EXERCISE 1A

1 (a) 14; (b) 24; (c) 4; (d) 18; (e) −16;
  (f) 25; (g) 105; (h) 46.2; (i) −35; (j) 12.

EXERCISE 1B

1 (a) 7; (b) 7; (c) 16; (d) 4;
  (e) 7; (f) 84; (g) 43.

2 (a) 5.39; (b) 5.39; (c) 8; (d) 2;
  (e) 5.39; (f) 25.3; (g) 35.9.

3 (a) 7, 41, 6.40;
  (b) 12, 225, 15;
  (c) 8, 36, 6;
  (d) 10, 50, 7.07;
  (e) 6.5, 263.25, 16.2.

EXERCISE 1C

Interpolation has been used in normal tables. Answers without using interpolation will be accepted in the examination.

1 (a) Normal, mean 950 ml, variance 800;
  (b) Normal, mean 25 ml, variance 1300.

2 (a) Normal, mean 510 g, variance 375, 0.788;
  (b) 0.111.

3 (a) Normal mean 10 g, variance 20.5;
  (b) 0.986.

4 (a) 0.814; (b) 0.626; (c) 0.243.

5 (a) (i) 0.092, (ii) 22.8 min;
  (b) 22 min;
  (c) (i) Normal, mean −3 min, variance 58, (ii) 0.653;
  (d) Choose Blue Star as probability of catching train greater (0.0432 > 0.001 35).

6 **(a)** Normal, mean 158 1, variance 325;

  (b) 0.010;

  (c) 0.186;

  (d) 0.419.

7 **(a)** 0.645;

  (b) 7.6 mm, 0.3 mm;

  (c) Normal, mean 0.3 mm variance 0.34, 0.303;

  (d) **(i)** 7.5 mm, **(ii)** 8.55 mm.

8 **(a)** **(i)** 0.0968, **(ii)** 0.953;

  (b) 471–559 g;

  (c) 0.208.

9 **(a)** 0.669;

  (b) 125.9 s;

  (c) 130 s, 9.8 s;

  (d) 0.575;

  (e) Julie – greater probability of qualifying (0.0513 > 0.000 23).

10 **(a)** 0.773;

  (b) 0.628;

  (c) 2.80 kg;

  (d) 0.936;

  (e) Normal, mean 19.0 kg, variance 0.0408;

  (f) 18.7–19.4 kg.

11 **(a)** 0.599;

  (b) 11.7 kg;

  (c) 0.868;

  (d) Normal, mean 241 kg, variance 0.8, 0.241.

2 The exponential distribution

EXERCISE 2A

1 **(a)** 0.248;   **(b)** 0.424;   **(c)** 0.202;   **(d)** 0.865.

2 0.148.

3 **(a)** 0.713;

  (b) 0.382;

  (c) 0.0821.

4 **(a)** **(i)** 0.632, **(ii)** 0.408, **(iii)** 0.600, **(iv)** 0.174, **(v)** 0;

  (b) 200 m, 40 000.

5 **(a)** **(i)** 0.181, **(ii)** 0.0494, **(iii)** 0.203, **(iv)** 0.135;

  (b) **(i)** 50.3 hrs, **(ii)** 527 hrs, **(iii)** 1780 hrs, **(iv)** 3470 hrs;

  (c) **(i)** 5000 hrs, 5000 hrs, **(ii)** 5000 hrs, 527 hrs;

  (d) 0.829.

6 **(a)** **(i)** 0.148, **(ii)** 0.121, **(iii)** 0.202, **(iv)** 0.330;

  (b) **(i)** 250 hrs, 250 hrs, **(ii)** 250 hrs, 16.7 hrs;

  (c) 0.274.

7 **(a)** 3.60 min;

   (b) 0.3125;

   (c) **(i)** B $(0.3125 < 0.565)$ B more likely,

       (ii) A $(P(X < 6) = 1)$ A more likely.

EXERCISE 2B

1   21.11, 9.97, 5.64, 3.28.

2   15.74, 9.55, 5.79, 3.51, 5.41.

3 **(a)** 45.66, 28.98, 18.40, 11.68, 12.12, 8.17;

   (b) Quite good agreement between observed and expected – exponential adequate model.

4 **(a)** 25.65, 18.93, 24.30, 20.47, 8.65;

   (b) Fairly good agreement apart from 100–200 class where there is a big difference between observed and expected. Exponential model probably not adequate;

   (c) If lengths between leaks do not follow exponential distribution, then leaks per metre do not follow Poisson and so leaks do not occur at random.

5 **(a)** 23.70, 19.02, 15.26, 22.08, 26.65, 13.29;

   (b) Big difference between observed and expected frequencies. Bicycles may pass in groups, so not independent (or mean number of bicycles may vary according to time of day).

3 Estimation

EXERCISE 3A

1   (3.36–31.88).

2   (16.1–41.0).

3 **(a)** (155–1248);   **(b)** (124–2024).

4   (0.07–0.199), no as 0.06 is below lower limit.

5   (0.21–1.03), (0.0077–0.0213), no.

6 **(a)** **(i)** (96.6–258.2), **(ii)** (85.1–216.8);

   (b) Appears that mean has reduced but standard deviation is unchanged; agree with the manager's suggestion but, depending on costs of special investigations, the figure of £900 may be too high.

7 **(a)** (8.1–57.0);

   (b) $57 > 5^2$, no convincing evidence to support claim.

8 **(a)** (32.7–90.7);

   (b) **(i)** (2348–2399), **(ii)** (2330–2417);

   (c) CI(i) is probably preferable to CI(ii) because it uses extra information and a standard deviation of 35 is consistent with CI calculated in **(a)**. However, CI(ii) is valid even if $\sigma \neq 35$.

9 **(a)** Range of $72 - 17 = 55 \gg 6 \times \sigma = 24$;

   (b) (13.3–37.8), claim confirmed.

    (c) (28.8–53.2);

    (d) Unsuitable since, although mean appears the same, the variability is significantly greater.

10 (a) (i) (24.52–29.64), **(ii)** (1.52–5.98);

    (b) 10.61 kN, 7.40 kN, Regulation appears adequate as greatest load value is less than value of k which has at most only a 1% risk of failure.

4 Hypothesis testing: one-sample tests

Where the significance level is not specified in the question, 5% is used in the given answers. Other levels could be used.

EXERCISE 4A

1 $\chi^2 = 18.8$, c.v. 4.404 and 23.337, accept $\sigma = 2.5$ cm.

2 $\chi^2 = 17.2$, c.v. 19.675, no significant evidence that σ exceeds 2 kg.

3 $\chi^2 = 19.6$, assuming normal distribution c.v. 5.009 and 24.736, accept $\sigma = 20$ kg.

4 $\chi^2 = 5.70$, c.v. 23.685, no significant evidence that σ^2 exceeds 0.002 g^2.

5 $\chi^2 = 3.00$, c.v. 3.940, evidence that σ^2 exceeds 6.0, assuming distribution normal and the sample is random.

6 $\chi^2 = 5.53$, c.v. 2.733, no significant evidence that σ reduced.

EXERCISE 4B

1 $P(X \geqslant 10 \mid P = 0.6) = 0.0834$, insufficient evidence to support claim.

2 $P(X \geqslant 14 \mid P = 0.35) = 0.1263$, accept $p = 0.35$.

3 $P(X \geqslant 21 \mid P = 0.5) = 0.0214$, claim supported.

4 $P(X \leqslant 8 \mid \lambda = 12) = 0.1550$, no significant evidence that less than 2% damaged.

5 $z = 2.10$, c.v. ± 1.96, evidence $p \neq 40\%$ (more than 40% have double glazing.)

6 $z = 1.95$, c.v. 1.6449, evidence of improvement, assumed shots may be regarded as a random sample.

EXERCISE 4C

1 $P(X \leqslant 8 \mid \lambda = 12) = 0.1550$, accept mean $= 4$.

2 $P(X \leqslant 2 \mid \lambda = 3.7) = 0.2854$, no significant evidence of reduction.

3 $z = -2.03$, c.v. -2.3263, no significant evidence that mean less than 3.

4 $z = -2.18$, c.v. -1.6449, manager's announcement heeded.

5 $P(X \leqslant 9 \mid \lambda = 14) = 0.1094$, no significant evidence $\lambda < 2.8$.

6 (a) $z = -1.79$, c.v. ± 1.96, accept manufacturer's claim;

    (b) Random sample.

MIXED EXERCISE

1 (a) $\chi^2 = 38.7$, c.v. 4.404 and 23.337, conclude variance $\neq (>)35$;
   (b) $t = 1.30$, c.v. ± 2.179, accept $\mu = 60$, normal distribution assumed.

2 $z = -1$, c.v. ± 1.96, accept $p = 0.5$, if $p = 0.5$ P(5 correct) = 0.03125, advise continue.

3 $\chi^2 = 25.2$, c.v. 5.629 and 26.119, accept $\sigma = 12$ s.

4 $z = 1.83$, c.v. 1.6449, significant evidence $\mu > 3$.

5 (a) $\chi^2 = 21.3$, c.v. 7.562 and 30.191, accept $\sigma = 10$, normal
       distribution assumed;
   (b) $z = -1.89$, c.v. ± 1.96, accept $\mu = 75$.

6 $z = -2.38$, c.v. -1.6449, evidence mean < 4.

7 P$(X \geqslant 17 \mid p = 0.6) = 0.0160 < 0.05$, claim valid.

8 $\chi^2 = 16.9$, c.v. 2.700 and 19.023 accept $\sigma^2 = 0.005$, $z = -1.34$,
   c.v. ± 1.96, accept $\mu = 10$ or $t = 1.01$, c.v. ± 2.262, assume normal
   distribution.

9 $z = 1.22$, c.v. ± 1.96, accept $p = 70\%$, $t = -1.35$, c.v. ± 1.734, accept
   $\mu = 275$.

10 $\chi^2 = 12.8$, c.v. 1.237 and 14.449, accept not more variable, $z = -2.12$,
   c.v. ± 1.96, evidence readings biased.

11 0.68, $z = 3.27$, c.v. 1.6449, conclude $> 60\%$ contain driver only.

12 $\chi^2 = 14.0$, c.v. 0.831 and 12.833, conclude variability changed
   (increased), $t = 0.52$, c.v. ± 2.571, accept no change, assume random
   sample from normal distribution.

13 $t = -3.62$, c.v. -1.833, conclude operation improved.

14 (a) (i) $\chi^2 = 39.2$, c.v. 1.69 and 16.93, σ changed (increased),
         (ii) $t = 2.57$, c.v. ± 2.365, mean changed (increased);
   (b) Other factors – notably the weather – will vary between years.

15 (a) $\chi^2 = 13.5$, c.v. 1.237 and 14.449, accept $\sigma = 10$ s;
   (b) $t = -1.48$, c.v. ± 2.447, accept $\mu = 240$ s
       or $z = -2.23$, c.v. ± 1.96, $\mu \neq 240$ s (< 240 s).

16 $t = 2.30$, c.v. ± 2.045, mean $\neq 200$ g (> 200 g),
   P$(X \geqslant 6 \mid p = 0.15) = 0.2894$, accept $p = 15\%$.

17 (a) P$(X \geqslant 13 \mid \lambda = 7) = 0.0270$, mean > 1 per day;
   (b) $z = -0.33$, c.v. ± 1.96, accept $p = 40\%$.

18 $\chi^2 = 15.0$, c.v. 1.237 and 14.449, $\sigma \neq 30$ (> 30),
   $t = -1.48$, c.v. ± 2.447, accept $\mu = 2400$.

19 P$(X \leqslant 11 \mid p = 0.4) = 0.0709 > 0.025$, accept $p = 40\%$.

5 Hypothesis testing: two-sample tests

EXERCISE 5A

1 $F = 1.39$, c.v. 4.200, accept variances equal.

2 $F = 4.21$, c.v. 3.102, evidence variance increased.

3 $F = 1.48$, c.v. 3.677, accept variances equal.

4 $F = 3.30$, c.v. 2.753, librarians more variable than designers, assumes samples random and distribution normal.

5 $F = 5.20$, c.v. 6.98, accept no differences in variability.

6 $F = 1.91$, c.v. 5.89, accept variances equal.

EXERCISE 5B

1 $z = 4.83$, c.v. ±1.96, accept no effect.

2 $z = -1.2$, c.v. ±1.96, accept no difference.

3 $z = 2.35$, c.v. ±1.96, significant evidence of difference – new line completes more crates.

4 $z = 1.68$, c.v. ±1.96, accept no difference.

5 (a) $z = -0.88$, c.v. ±1.96, no difference;

(b) $z = -2.06$, c.v. ±1.96, difference (trainees slower).

6 $z = 1.44$, c.v. ±1.96, accept Alison takes five minutes longer on average.

EXERCISE 5C

1 $t = 2.34$, c.v. ±2.179, mean times differ (B quicker).

2 $t = 2.52$, c.v. ±2.086, means differ (A higher).

3 $t = 3.09$, c.v. ±2.921.

4 $t = 1.88$, c.v. ±2.201, accept no difference.

5 $t = 2.10$, c.v. ±2.228, accept means equal.

6 (a) $F = 1.20$, c.v. 2.949, accept no difference in variability.

(b) $t = 0.702$, c.v. ±2.045, accept mean life has increased by five hours.

MIXED EXERCISE

1 $F = 2.7$, c.v. 3.330, accept no difference.

2 $F = 1.2$, c.v. 4.197, accept no difference.

3 $F = 3.80$, c.v. 5.523, accept variances the same.

4 $z = 0.615$, c.v. ±1.96, accept no difference.

5 $t = 2.61$, c.v. 1.812, Southville more expensive.

6 $z = 1.94$, c.v. 2.3263, accept no difference in mean mass gain. Mass gain may be affected by initial mass. A possible difference could have been masked by mass differences between groups.

7 (a) (i) $F = 1.40$, c.v. 6.85, accept no difference in variability.

(ii) $t = -0.60$, c.v. ±2.179, accept no difference in means;

(b) Reasonable to leave out 297 as caused by abnormal circumstances, normal distribution and equality of variances would have been violated if it had been included.

8 $z = -2.49$, c.v. $= -1.6449$, conclude W awards more marks than V.

9 $F = 1.75$, c.v. 3.665, accept variances equal, $t = -3.29$, c.v. ±2.08, means differ (variety 1 lighter). Answers unaffected by error in measuring device.

10 (a) $F = 5.63$, c.v. 6.85, accept variances equal;

   (b) $t = 3.43$, c.v. 1.782, mean lower below factory.

11 (a) $F = 1.37$, c.v. 6.85, accept variances equal;

   (b) $t = -0.61$, c.v. ± 2.179, accept no difference in means. Reasonable to leave out 99 as this was due to circumstances unlikely to be repeated. If included, assumptions of normal distribution and equal variances would have been violated.

12 $z = 0.91$, c.v. 1.6449, accept no increase in mean score. Large samples mean s can be used as estimate of σ, also the means will be approximately normally distributed even if individual scores are not.

13 (a) $F = 1.12$, c.v. 4.020, accept variances equal;

   (b) $t = -0.90$, c.v. -1.734, no increase.

14 (a) $t = 1.42$, c.v. 2.353, A not more than 114;

   (b) $F = 2.30$, c.v. 14.88, accept standard deviations equal;

   (c) $t = -0.91$, c.v. ± 2.306, accept means equal.

15 (a) $F = 1.33$, c.v. 5.988, accept variance equal;

   (b) $t = 4.45$, c.v. ± 2.201, assistant quicker; different designs should be compared by same person, make conditions, e.g. time of day when shaving takes place, as standard as possible.

16 (a) Variances unknown, but may be assumed equal;

   (b) (ii) $z = 1.59$, c.v. ± 1.96, accept no difference,
   (iii) Large sample.

17 (a) $F = 2.25$, c.v. 2.78 (using interpolation), accept no difference in variability;

   (b) $t = 2.27$, c.v. ± 2.042, means different (A greater).

18 (a) All tea bags of same brand weighed by same analyst although two analysts participated;

   (b) Values of s are similar for each brand of tea bag;

   (c) $t = 0.89$, c.v. ± 2.074, accept means equal;

   (d) Variances unaffected, pooled estimate valid, $t = 3.66$, c.v. ± 2.074, means different (A heavier).

6 Testing for goodness of fit

The test statistic may vary slightly depending on whether 2 or more than 2 d.p. are kept for the Es. Also whether tables or calculators are used for the normal distribution.

EXERCISE 6A

1 4.170, test statistic (t.s.) 4.23, c.v. 12.592, accept Poisson.

2 t.s. 5.89, c.v. 3.841, reject binomial.

3 (a) t.s. 5.65, c.v. 9.488, accept claim;

   (b) Expected values for D and E would have been less than 5. It would be necessary to pool these two classes.

4 t.s. 0.114, c.v. 5.991, accept binomial; binomial implies probability of each student answering each question correctly is the same.

5 t.s. 150, c.v. 13.277, reject Poisson.

6 t.s. 5.52, c.v. 12.592, accept average number served per hour is constant.

7 t.s. 5.87, c.v. 11.070, accept B(7, 0.5).

8 (a) t.s. 14.6, c.v. 5.991, reject Poisson;

(b) Not Poisson, implies not distributed at random.

9 t.s. 179, c.v. 9.488, age distribution not consistent with women living in Manchester.

10 (a) t.s. 110, c.v. 11.345, reject Poisson;

(b) Not Poisson, implies not random with constant mean rate.

EXERCISE 6B

1 t.s. 13.7, c.v. 7.815, reject normal.

2 t.s. 3.21, c.v. 13.77, accept model adequate.

3 t.s. 15.6, c.v. 14.067, reject exponential.

4 50.3, 2.66, t.s. 4.22, c.v. 6.635, accept normal, adequate model.

5 t.s. 4.37, c.v. 11.070, reject exponential.

6 (a) t.s. 11.9, c.v. 9.488, reject normal;

(b) Biggest discrepancies from normal are classes 35–39 and 40–49. This could have been due to moving scripts from 35–39 to 40–49 on review. Could repeat the test combining these two classes.

7 (b) t.s. 3.39, c.v. 9.48, accept exponential.

MIXED EXERCISE

1 (a) t.s. 20.2, c.v. 16.919, reject uniform distribution;

(b) Appear to be more errors on Mondays and Fridays than in the middle of the week.

2 (a) t.s. 10.7, c.v. 7.815, reject normal;

(b) Mill appears to remove (nearly) all lengths below 67 m to avoid paying compensation; this may be the reason for normal not providing an adequate model.

3 t.s. 9.55, c.v. 7.815, reject binomial; implies not independent of surgeon.

4 (a) t.s. 41.8, c.v. 12.592, reject Poisson;

(b) t.s. 3.50, c.v. 11.07, accept Poisson, mean 3;

(c) Poisson accepted in **(b)** implies serious blemishes occur at random at a constant average rate. Rejection in **(a)** due to reduction of strings to five in lengths which initially contained more than five strings.

5 (a) t.s. 0.14, c.v. 5.991, accept binomial;

(b) t.s. 0.40, c.v. 7.815, accept Poisson;

(c) The fits are suspiciously good. Both test statistics are in the lower 10% of the χ^2 distribution. The probability of this occurring by chance is less than 0.01. Strong evidence to support suspicions.

6 (a) 2.5;

(b) t.s. 2.81, c.v. 11.07, accept model is appropriate (or t.s. 1.72, c.v. 9.488 if $E = 4.98$ pooled).

7 (a) (i) 71.49–72.24,
(ii) 67.3–76.5;

(b) t.s. 26.2, c.v. 9.488 (or t.s. 13.7, c.v. 7.815 if $E = 4.92$ pooled), reject normal;

(c) Sample in **(a) (i)** large so result reliable even if distribution not normal; result in **(a) (ii)** refers to individual pieces and so unreliable as distribution not normal.

7 Testing the parameter β of the regression equation

EXERCISE 7A

The answers are generally given to 3 s.f. even where more than 3 s.f. will be needed at a later stage of the calculation.

1 (a) 154;

(b) $t = 11.1$, c.v. 4.032, reject $\beta = 0$.

2 (a) 11.2;

(b) $t = 7.55$, c.v. 2.447, reject $\beta = 0$.

3 (a) 0.159;

(b) $t = -10.5$, c.v. -2.132, conclude $\beta < 0$.

4 (a) $t = 5.81$, c.v. 2.365, reject $\beta = 0$;

(b) $t = 0.0270$, c.v. 2.365, accept $\beta = 0$;

(c) $t = -4.60$, c.v. -2.998, conclude $\beta < 0.9$.

5 (b) $y = 0.389x - 0.142$;

(c) 0.0845;

(d) $t = 51.9$; c.v. 2.365, reject $\beta = 0$;

(e) Temperature will depend on time;

(f) Good fit over observed values; cannot continue indefinitely.

6 (b) $y = 81.2 + 0.621x$;

(c) Points well scattered, some quite large residuals, no particular pattern;

(d) 320;

(e) $t = 2.08$, c.v. 2.228, accept $\beta = 0$;

(f) There appears to be considerable variation in the yield but there is insufficient evidence to attribute any of this variation to the temperature.

7 (b) $y = 0.246 + 1.09x$;

(c) $t = 1.78$, c.v. 3.250, accept $\beta = 1$;

(d) Clearly estimate may depend on actual age but actual cannot depend on estimate. Hence, choice of estimate as dependent variable is correct. Since the intercept is small (0.246) and $\beta = 1$ has been accepted the data is consistent with the model $y = x + \varepsilon$, that is, the estimate is the actual age plus a random error. This may not be the exact model but there is little evidence of any bias in the estimates.

8 (b) $y = 0.776 + 0.0213x$;

(c) No pattern to the residuals although some are quite large;

(d) 0.2005;

(e) $t = 1.16$, c.v. 2.306, accept $\beta = 0$;

(f) Concentration of final product may depend on amount of chemical used but amount cannot depend on concentration. Hence, choice of concentration as dependent variable is correct. There is considerable variation in the final concentration but insufficient evidence to show that any of this can be explained by the amount of chemical used.

9 (b) $t = 4.05$, c.v. 2.365, reject $\beta = 0$;

(c) The seventh Saturday – takings way below those predicted by the model;

(d) Most points lie close to line. Without the abnormal point identified in **(c)** they would be closer still. No particular pattern to residuals – the one large one has been explained. Model appears valid – apart from the seventh Saturday and there is a reason for this. Model also plausible as you would expect an increase in takings with more staff;

(e) $y = 291 + 2.02x$, $t = 9.98$, c.v. 2.447, reject $\beta = 0$;

(f) Part **(e)** confirms numerically the conclusion drawn in **(d)** that there is even stronger evidence of a linear relationship between takings and number of part-time staff if the seventh Saturday is excluded. There is some suggestion in the scatter diagram that this may not apply for larger values of x and the model should not be extrapolated. The number of part-time staff is increased each week so it is possible that there is another reason for the increase in takings – such as the approach of Christmas.

10 (b) $y = 686 + 48.5x$, y clearly dependent since hours open cannot depend on receipts;

(d) β is an estimate of the increase in takings for each additional hour the bar is open.

(e) $t = 1.47$, c.v. 1.943, accept $\beta = 40$;

(f) There is strong visual evidence from the scatter diagram that takings increase if bar open longer but there is insufficient evidence to establish that takings exceed £40 per hour. Increasing the opening hours may not be worth while financially.

Exam style practice paper

1 Insufficient evidence to substantiate the claim (0.0769 > 0.05).

2 (a) 0.186;

(b) 200, 200.

3 $-1.79 < -1.6449$, evidence that injuries reduced.

4 (a) Assume normal distribution, 42.9–188;

(b) s.d. 10 → variance 100. This is contained in confidence interval. No conclusive evidence that s.d. does not need 10.

5 (a) All variety P measured by inspector A and all variety Q by inspector B. Any differences could be due to varieties or inspectors. Could have been avoided by the same inspector measuring both varieties.

(b) $F = 1.23$, c.v. 3.209, accept no difference in variability;

(c) $t = 2.22$, c.v. 1.714, conclude mean weight of variety P exceeds that of Q.

6 (a) $y = 75.9 + 1.29x$;

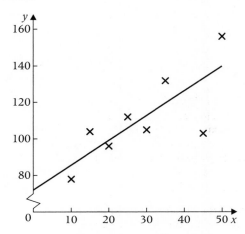

(b) (i) 230,

(ii) $t = 3.17$, c.v. $= 1.943$, conclude pulse rate increase with number of step-ups;

(c) No obvious pattern to residuals and no outliers. Hence assumption of $N(0, \sigma^2)$ is plausible. Pulse rate is measured for predetermined number of step-ups so model is entirely appropriate.

Index

alternative hypothesis 34
answers to examples 133–143

binomial distribution
    cumulative function tables
        121–125
    goodness of fit, degrees of
        freedom **84**
binomial population proportion
    hypothesis testing 38–41–**42**–43

Central Limit Theorem 20
χ^2 (chi-squared) distribution 26
    degrees of freedom **79**
    percentage points table 130
confidence intervals and limits
    background 25
    normal population standard
        deviation 25–**26**–27–29
    normal population variance
        25–**26**–27–29
continuous distributions
    goodness of fit tests 87–89–**90**–
        91–**92**–93–96
    probability 1
continuous random variables
    mean **2–3**
    variance 2, **4–5**
critical region 34
critical value 34
cumulative distribution function,
    exponential distribution **16**–17–20

degrees of freedom 26
    binomial distribution fit **84**
    χ^2 (chi-squared) distribution **79**
    exponential fit **90**
    normal distribution fit **92**
    Poisson fit **82**
dependent variable 103
discrete distributions, goodness of fit
    tests 80–81–**82**–83–87
discrete random variables
    mean **2–3**
    variance 2, **4–5**

estimation 25–33
    key point summary 32
examination style paper 117–119,
    answers 142–143
explanatory variable 103
exponential distribution 15–24
    cumulative distribution
        function **16**–17–20
    fitting to observed data 20–23
    goodness of fit, degrees of
        freedom 90
    intervals between successive
        Poisson events 15, **16**
    key point summary 23
    mean **15**
    probability density function **15**
    standard deviation **15**

F-distribution 56
    percentage points table 131–132
    variance equality test 65
Fisher, R A 56

goodness of fit tests 79–101
    background **79**
    continuous distributions 87–89–
        90–91–**92**–93–96
    discrete distributions 80–81–**82**–
        83–87
    key point summary 100
goodness of fit, degrees of freedom
    binomial distribution **84**
    exponential distribution **90**
    normal distribution **92**
    Poisson distribution **82**

hypothesis testing
    background 34–35
    β regression parameter 103–115
    binomial population
        proportion 38–41–**42**–43
    normal population variance
        36–37–38
    one-sample tests 34–54
    one-sample tests key point
        summary 51

Poisson population mean 43–**44**–45

student's *t*-test **35**–36

t-test **35**–36

two normal population means (variances known) 59–**60**–61–64

two normal population means (variances unknown) 64–**65**–66–68

two normal population means for equality or difference **60**–61–62

two normal population variances 55–**56**–57–59

two populations parameters 55

two-sample tests 55–78

two-sample tests key point summary 75–76

independent normal variables, linear combinations 1–14

independent random variables, variance **4–5**

key point summaries
estimation 32
exponential distribution 23
goodness of fit tests 100
hypothesis testing one-sample tests 51
hypothesis testing two-sample tests 75–76
linear combinations of independent random variables 13
regression tests for β parameter 114

linear combinations of independent normal variables 1–14
key point summary 13
normal distribution **6**

mean
continuous random variables **2–3**
discrete random variables **2–3**
exponential distribution **15**
Poisson distribution hypothesis testing 43–**44**–45
two normal populations (variances known) 59–**60**–61–64
two normal populations (variances unknown and unequal) 65
two normal populations (variances unknown but equal) 64–**65**–66–68

two normal populations for equality or difference of means 60–61–62

normal distribution
goodness of fit, degrees of freedom **92**
percentage points tables 125
population standard deviation confidence intervals 25–**26**–27–29
population variance confidence intervals 25–**26**–27–29
population variance hypothesis testing **36**–37–38
tables 124

notation
RSS 104
S_{xx} 103

null hypothesis 34

one-sample tests, hypothesis testing 34–54

one-tailed test 35

percentage points of the normal distribution tables 128

Poisson distribution
cumulative function tables 126
goodness of fit, degrees of freedom **82**
population mean hypothesis testing 43–**44**–45

predictor variable 103

probability density function 1–2
exponential distribution **15**

regression
background 103
hypothesis tests for β parameter 103–115
simple linear 103–**104**–105
testing hypothesis about β parameter 105–106–**107**–108–113
tests for β parameter, key point summary 114

residual 106

response variable 103

RSS notation 105

significance level 35

Snedecor, G W 56

standard deviation, exponential distribution **15**

statistical tables
binomial cumulative distribution function 121–125

χ^2 (chi-squared) distribution
percentage points 130
F-distribution percentage points
131–132
normal distribution function 127
normal distribution percentage
points 128
percentage points of student's
t-distribution 129
percentage points of the
F-distribution 131–132
percentage points of the normal
distribution 128
percentage points of the χ^2
(chi-squared) distribution 130
Poisson cumulative distribution
function 126
student's t-distribution percentage
points 129
t-distribution percentage points
129
student's t-distribution percentage
points table 129
student's t-test, hypothesis testing
35–36
S_{xx} notation 104

t-distribution percentage points table
129
t-test
hypothesis testing **35–36**
two normal populations means
(variances unknown and
unequal)
65
test statistic 34
two normal population means
hypothesis testing (variances
known) 59–**60**–61–64
hypothesis testing (variances
unknown) 64–**65**–66–68
hypothesis testing for equality or
difference **60**–61–62
two normal population variances,
hypothesis testing 55–**56**–57–59
two populations parameters,
hypothesis testing 55

two-sample tests, hypothesis testing
55–78
two-tailed test 35
type 1 error 34
type 2 error 34

variance
continuous random variables 2,
4–5
discrete random variables 2, **4–5**
independent random variables
4–5
two normal populations 55–**56**–
57–59

worked examples
baking smell 65–66
biscuit manufacture 7–8
brewing grain 28–29
bus rush hour travel 27
cucumbers in brine 109–110
drug test on patients 39–40
dustbin bag production 40
electrical component lifetime 18
examination marks analysis
92–94
garage modernisation 44
generator breakdown intervals
21–22
hamburger fat content 90–92
hockey scoring practice 82–84
hot drinks dispensers comparison
57, 67
jam jar production 6
lorry fuel consumption 107–109
monitor watching 17
motorway accidents 81–82
plastic plate strains 105–107
river water alkalinity 61–62
rubber ball production 6–7
shareholder sampling 41–42
steakburgers fat content 35–36
steel wire breaking strength 36–37
taxi waiting times 87–88
thread faults 43
white car intervals 89–90